LET'S WRECK

Psychobilly Flashbacks From The Eighties & Beyond

CRAIG BRACKENRIDGE

STORMSCREEN PRODUCTIONS
2nd edition

To I, P & F for putting up with Daddio!

First published in the United Kingdom in 2003 by
STORMSCREEN PRODUCTIONS
Retford
Nottinghamshire DN22 0JL.
2nd edition, 2005.

ISBN 0-9546249-0-4

Author's Note

To avoid any confusion before you turn another page, please note, this book was written initially for true fans of Psychobilly and as such I have (whenever possible) attempted to avoid stating the bleedin' obvious. I have assumed that this hunk of pulp (non) fiction is mainly of interest to psychobillies old and new and therefore saw no point in including inches of text explaining things such as who The Meteors are, how influential the Klub Foot was, where and when exactly the Hemsby weekenders were, etc, etc.

I apologise to any casual reader who may be bamboozled by certain references but this tome is only intended to reminisce and reflect on the cult of Psychobilly from one perspective (mine). The facts, dates and discographies of the movement should be reserved for a more definitive 'encyclopedia' of Psychobilly. Now there's an idea!

It was a sweaty Glasgow night in the late 1980'S and The Meteors were in town. The city's Technical College Student's Union was bouncing. Hundreds of psychobillies were battling it out on the dancefloor. Ex-punks, teds, skins, rockabillies and some desperate fad chasing poseurs were now quiffed up, dressed down and soaking up the glorious noise of the Godfathers of Psychobilly. The scene was at its peak, the gig was long sold out and even goths and rugby-playing lunkheads were getting into it.

In the centre, at the front, was a mass of writhing bodies. Stomping. Wrecking. Gleefully punching fuck out of each other and loving every moment. I was there, laughing through the pain barrier, pissed and listening to one of my favourite bands knocking out high-speed, furious, Rock 'n' Roll while trading punches with dozens of like-minded mates. In heaven.

As the music relentlessly kept its pace I stumbled and fell forward but was then pushed back onto my feet. That was the theme of the wrecking pit, hit 'em till they drop but don't let them fall. But this time I reached standing position then continued to fall backwards. Again, someone came to my aid and I was propelled forward but I fell like a tree - face first. I cracked my head on... the floor? A beer glass? Someone's steel-toecapped boot? I was picked up and I staggered from the dancefloor.

My head was cold and wet, 'Some dirty bastard has thrown beer on me'. But it was not beer and as I wiped my head I noticed the blood. It was soaking me. My friends dragged me down to the toilet and I saw myself in the mirror. The prom scene in 'Carrie' sprung to mind. I laughed out of bravado then dropped onto a chair and asked my mate if I was going to die. An ambulance took me to hospital, 'He's been drinking - probably fighting'. No anaesthetic. Thirteen stitches. BAM! Welcome to the wrecking crew!

Pure vinyl dementia! Early signs of a misspent youth.
Any cash was spent on booze, hairspray and (of course) records.

My transition into a fully fledged Psychobilly was almost overnight. Before my introduction to King Kurt and The Meteors in the early Eighties, I was a shambling indie type with a love for The Smiths and Echo & the Bunnymen. Previously I had dabbled a bit with Punk, then Mod and (alarmingly) a brief dalliance with electropop such as Gary Numan and A Flock of Seagulls. But that is probably just the way of all spotty teenagers, the elusive search to belong in between bouts of frantic wanking.

My pre-psychobilly image consisted of a large floppy quiff, long at the sides and back, held in place with dollops of cheapo gel. Almost like a seventies-Ted type barnet but without the greasiness. I constantly wore an old navy blue raincoat which reached down to my knees, junk shop trousers and (always, always, always) a T-shirt & V-neck jumper combination. I drank cider (always bought for me because of my youthful looks), smoked roll-ups & joints and consistently kept an eye out for young indie birds. Shy, sensitive... my arse!

When the psycho bug first bit all that clobber hit the bin immediately. And it all began one night in 1983 when I was parked in front of the box for my weekly fix of 'Top of the Pops'. Having always been a big music fan, and in a time before MTV and multi-channel viewing, TOTP was essential viewing and almost the only way to see music on British TV. Despite the lack of many decent bands on the show, I still tuned in religiously even if only to yell abuse at the screen when pish bands like Black Lace and Modern Romance made an appearance.

That particular evening the line-up was poor as ever until

Earliest photo of a Psychobilly convert, 1984.

King Kurt appeared performing 'Destination Zululand'. Pre-empting their messy live performances the tight-sphinctered BBC studio boffins had covered their set in plastic sheeting. Kurt bounced around the stage, looking slightly out of place on a clinically clean studio set, but still tearing up the place in a blur of boots and quiffs. I was gobsmacked. After endless parades of pampered, powdered ponces over the years I could not believe TOTP had allowed these rowdy bumpkins onto the show. To this day I have only seen that performance once (our family was late in embracing the video boom, and even then we bought a betamax recorder) and while the content of the performance is a bit misty, the feeling it gave me was so powerful I still remember it clearly. Whatever the fuck this was I had to be part of it and for a rare occasion in my life I was stunned into silence (temporarily).

I saw King Kurt's TOTP appearance on the Thursday night and by Friday I was in the barber's chair demanding a flat-top. After gassing excitedly with my mates about King Kurt's unique TV appearance, I made a quick trip to the jeans warehouse for trousers and nipped into Millets for a tartan shirt and boots. I was not well versed in the do's and dont's of Psychobilly couture but it felt like the right thing to do and one of the consistent joys of psycho fashion has always been the cheapness of the clobber, which was ideal for a cash-strapped teen like myself.

New Haircut, new T-shirt and fledgling beer-belly, 1984.

I never felt like a bandwagon jumper because I just knew this was what I had been waiting for - Rock 'n' Roll, Punk and general rowdiness all rolled into one. Subconsciously I must have picked up some early buzz on this new scene through the music press which I dug into regularly and, although I have no recollection, I am sure I must have seen a few early psychos cutting about the streets of Glasgow. Whatever the reason, I sensed that a Psychobilly explosion was brewing and I wanted to be part of it. I was not alone as my mates Gaz and Stix joined along with me and we hooked up with a few other locals with the same ideas, including my now long-term amigo Raymie. In Cumbernauld, a concrete-clad New Town on the outskirts of Glasgow, a new Psychobilly community was evolving.

Not long after I had first been introduced to Psychobilly by King Kurt, my mate's girlfriend Lorraine sent me further on the road to wreck and ruin. She was a student at Dundee's School of Art who we visited frequently. Despite being a devotee of yank weirdoes Devo, she was heavily into the blossoming psycho scene especially The Cramps and The Meteors. At that time I knew little of either of the bands but she soon set me straight.

I vividly remember coming home in the bus, after a weekend at her place, and listening to The Meteors 'Wrecking Crew' album all the way. It blew me away, I was so excited I felt as if I was on speed and fidgeted wildly all the way home. It was just the blast of high speed Rock 'n' Roll, that I had been waiting for. When I tracked down The Meteors 'In Heaven' the buzz was even more powerful and it gave me a real sense of something big happening. From that point on I hunted down as many Psychobilly sounds as I could with the same passion as a greedy bastard on the scent of fresh pies.

THE RAZORBACKS

More time was spent creating The Razorbacks logo than writing new songs.

The Razorbacks, live at The Scabaret, Cumbernauld (1985).

Around the time of my earliest introduction to Psychobilly, two school friends and I were in a band - a new experience for all of us. We were called The Evil Doods and, in an attempt to appear exotic, we adopted "wacky" stage names to disguise our lack of talent. I was the singer, Stitch Beermat, the drummer was my best mate, Stix 'O' Wood (aka MaCaque), and our guitarist Gaz revelled in the monicker of Wes Trousers. It was standard bedroom punk with a touch of goth but also (way ahead of our time) using tape loops and samples.

In the spring of 1985, after a string of local gigs, we managed to secure an early gig at the Dundee Art School and The Evil Doods were at last on the road. For us this was a biggy as we were assured that Dundee's flat-top contingent would be there in force and this would be our first toehold in the burgeoning Psychobilly scene. The evening would feature us live plus a night full of psycho, goth and alternative sounds.

Dundee, for those readers unaware of the city, was quite a dark, overbearing place in the early eighties. It has been fancified recently as a 'City of Discovery' but in those days it was like the black hole of Calcutta. For some reason this dark heart of Scotland was home to an alarming number of hardcore psychobillies, a crew whose huge quiffs and masses of tattoos seemed long established despite the relative youthfulness of the scene. These guys were psycho to the core when King Kurt and The Meteors were releasing their debut albums. Maybe they were caught in a weird time-loop or maybe my memory is a bit fucked-up (you decide) but either way these geezers must have been amongst Scotland's Psychobilly pioneers. For that reason we felt the need to impress up in Dundee but we failed to take two key factors into account:

a. We were a shite band live.
b. We were not (as yet) really Psychobilly.

As a young band we had played locally many times but (and here is a tip for all you young rockers out there) your friends almost always say you played well, even when your performance was tripe.

With this false assumption that we were actually a competent live act, we took to the stage with a half-baked concoction of Rock 'n'

Roll covers and self-penned songs with no real structure. The majority of tunes ended with a cacophony of guitars and drums and me on my back screaming into the mike. After this pitiful performance the Dundee psychos welcomed us with open fists, and were so furious at our poor facsimile of Psychobilly that they started fighting amongst themselves during the gig as a warm-up to unleashing their fury on us when we came offstage. We were literally hounded out of the venue and had bottles thrown at us as we bundled our gear into the van and headed back to Cumbernauld in shame.

After the embarrassment of 'The Evil Doods' in Dundee, Stix and I were more determined than ever to follow the Psychobilly template more closely which meant Gaz returned to the bedroom, while we hooked up with a couple of old school friends Ali and Kev (aka Kev Redneck).

Ali was a bedroom guitarist of astounding ability but minimal stagecraft. He could "play guitar like ringin' a bell" but would rarely move anything other than his hands on stage and never looked at the audience. Kev was, then, in the formative stages of his music career but slapped his (electric) bass like a natural born rocker. A mere month after The Evil Doods demise The Razorbacks were formed and we played our first local gigs over the New Year holiday period of 1986.

Early snap of The Razorbacks, Cumbernauld Theatre, 1985.

Initially we were no more than a covers band on speed, knocking out high-velocity versions of 'Johnny Be Good', 'Purple Haze', 'Shake, Rattle and Roll', and the Cliff & the Shadows gem 'We Say Yeah'. I tore up the stage, arsing around while disguising my limited singing ability by yelling fast 'n' hard. Stix bashed his huge kit almost fanatically, often singing and dancing while still playing. Kev threw a multitude of rock star shapes while Ali rarely moved from behind his amp but noodled on his guitar with astounding precision.

We initially played around our local patch of Cumbernauld, mostly as the house band of an alternative variety club, Scabaret, run by comedian Stu 'Who' Henderson. It often saw us lined up alongside fire-eaters, no-hopers and a few future stars such as Craig Ferguson and Coatbridge crooners Hue & Cry. Despite now having a reputation as a cultural blackspot twinned with Kabul, in the mid-eighties Cumbernauld had a thriving alternative music scene with a broad range of punters happy enough to indulge themselves in our psycho-versions of classic rock anthems. When we played we also attracted the small Psychobilly contingent which populated Cumbernauld and surrounding areas such as Kilsyth, Croy and Denny. A six man wrecking pit was occasionally present during the more rowdy moments of our set, leaving the rest of the audience bemused as our mates would pummel each other for three minute intervals then chat matily between songs.

Though a far more accomplished and musically adept act than The Evil Doods, The Razorbacks were still some way from true Psychobilly. As Kev and Ali were determinedly un-psycho, our range of covers had a wider appeal to music-starved punks, goths, hippies and local winos. Although I was keen to pursue a more puritan Psychobilly direction, Ali was not ready for a lifestyle change and Kev resolutely remained his own man. Stix was keen for a more psycho sound but recoiled with horror when I suggested he trim down his nine-piece, heavy-metal-overload drum kit into a more Rockabilly-based bass drum, floor tom and snare combination.

Nevertheless, I always enjoyed Razorbacks gigs as we had a fine blend of covers and original tunes which always guaranteed a good time. Another bonus was the fact that as Ali was such a motionless guitarist it gave me the chance to mime some strumming on an old guitar of mine, which was tastefully hand-decorated with the exclamation 'Wipeout' across it. It gave me the chance to dick around and show off some bogus noodling. The way I saw it was that the folks had paid for good rockin' entertainment, so they got Ali's quality sound accompanied by my frantic guitarmanship. I even went so far as to have a guitar lead from my axe disappearing somewhere behind the amps. It occasionally came loose and betrayed my fake twanging but nobody seemed to mind. It also helped me cover up the 'dead time' when I was not singing and allowed us to do some classic surf instrumentals, such as 'Pipeline', without me standing around like a spare prick.

Also on the scene at this stage were a band from Stirling called Four Walls Shaking. I know very little about them, as I saw them only once when we supported them in concert, but they made a massive impression on me. They played a hugely entertaining (and technically psycho-tastic) set, at Stirling's expansive Albert Halls which left me unsatisfied with The Razorbacks more mainstream sound. I think they supported The Meteors during their 'Wrecking Crew' tour of Scottish backwaters but as far as other gigs and record releases go - 'I know nothing'.

One of the reasons they perhaps failed to play a bigger part in Psychobilly history may have been their notoriously unfriendly Stirling following. At that Albert Halls gig, one hot summer evening in June 1986, a busload of Cumbernauld folks had followed us to the venue to offer support. The locals started on them almost immediately as they entered the hall, faces were punched, arses were kicked and a few blades were brandished. Hugely outnumbered, our followers eventually beat a hasty retreat during our set leaving us to make our own way home. After they left, with no incomers to pummel, the Stirling hayseeds started bashing each other. Luckily our appearance went down well and we had a great night but I still remember the whole evening carried the atmosphere of a wild west saloon brawl. Other towns which offered a similar warm beating were Coatbridge, Greenock and Paisley... and not a groupie in sight.

The following day, almost as a way of thanking our put upon fans, The Razorbacks played their finest gig at an open-air concert on some waste ground behind Cumbernauld College. This allowed the folks that had travelled to the Albert Halls the chance to relax, watch the band, and look for any stray Stirling punters to kick the shit out of.

Around the time of The Razorbacks, Cumbernauld boasted one other Psychobilly band, The Tombstones. They were a youthful trio of ex-skins who were immaculately be-quiffed and authentically psycho, sticking to a rigid Cramps/Meteors structure. I had heard them in our earliest band days as they practised at the same community centre as us on Friday nights. We never really spoke much at the time, as I am sure they regarded us as a half-arsed troop of wannabe psychobillies, but eventually we got together as mates when we appeared on the same bill at Cumbernauld district's biggest ever soundclash of street music.

The infamous Kilsyth 'anarchy nights' are legend for those old enough to remember them and really were a blip in the area's musical landscape. For two nights only, Kilsyth (a small hillbilly outpost in the west of Scotland) held a showcase of local Punk, Psychobilly and Oi bands in a dilapidated football club function suite. These days you could probably fit all of the region's street music faithful in the back of a Vauxhall Viva but for those two nights local headbangers were treated to an embarrassment of riches.

On the first night we were just visitors, heading into bandit country with The Tombstones and other Cumbernauld 'billies. Even though we only stayed a few miles from Kilsyth, this was my first trip into hayseed hell. To celebrate, I got gassed on Buckfast on the bus and put my fist through a nearby sports centre window. Ah, the dopey bravado of youth!

At the gig it was sheer splendour - punks, psychos, goths, skins and lots of alternative ladies. I had never seen the like, so many like-minded folk in the same place, and I enjoyed the gig so much I have absolutely no recollection of the bands that played. The main thing was that this was proof that a street music scene was booming in my own backyard and I had to be part of it.

At that very night my Psychobilly life took an even more important turn when I met some local Kilsyth geezers. They were a trio of bumpkins around the same point as myself in embracing the new Psychobilly movement and we soon got talking. Although one of them was a growler and seemed to want to kick my cunt in, the other two were friendly. They were then known as Rog, Stuart and Alan but were destined to be renamed Bob - The Black Puma, Tripney and Big Bert (don't ask!). We soon became good mates and from that point on they were alongside me almost every step of the way as I continued my psycho odyssey.

At the second (and final) Kilsyth anarchy night, a month or so later, The Razorbacks were on the bill along with: The Tombstones, a deadly serious Oi band and the gig organiser's Punk collective. Yet again there was a great turnout but this time the 'anarchy' vibe was even more strong and the place quickly became littered with broken glass, smashed furniture and the dog ends of joints. We seemed to go down a storm and loved playing to this rowdy audience so much that the bouncers forcibly ejected us from the stage when we refused to go off.

Towards the end of the set, I noticed one of the venue's boneheads motioning to me to say my goodnights. Instead, I shouted to the drummer to kick into our version of the classic instrumental floorshaker 'Wipeout' and we kept going. The staff turned the lights on, hauled us offstage and dragged us out the fire exit. Our gear followed close behind. By the time the club's owners realised how much damage had been done to the venue the Kilsyth Rangers' band nights were over for good - anarchy indeed!

In the end, we had the T-shirts, a cracking logo (a pig with a huge quiff) and a fully lettered-up 'tour' van (Stix' mini-bus) but we never really got anywhere. We had a brief spell when Kev left, well a few rehearsals, with a double-bass player called Tally. He was a cracking slap bassist with real Rockabilly roots but alongside the Razorback blend of Classic Rock, Metal and Rock 'n' Roll it just did not work and Kev returned to the fold for our final few gigs. Too noisy for normal folks but not really fitting the, then rigid, Psychobilly template, eventually we all lost interest. Many years later I came across a yank band of the same name at a Psychobilly festival. They were an excellent Rock 'n' Roll band with a healthy selection of record releases so our spell as The Razorbacks will forever remain a micro-footnote in psycho history.

For a short while Stix and I teamed up with Walter and Smiffy from The Tombstones (almost a Cumbernauld psycho-supergroup) and indulged our shared love of Trash in a band called The Electric Fits. This was an excellent idea but for some reason, which I have no recollection of, it came to nothing. Another Trash band, Mission Impossible, followed but again I have great trouble piecing together the past, probably because all band members were puffing weed like it was going out of fashion. So let that be a warning to all you teen-tokers out there, short-term memory loss can be a terrible... sorry, what was I saying?

While this whole experience may seem small potatoes in the UK Psychobilly scene it is important to remember that a bum-crack, small town like Kilsyth had probably not had an event of that kind before and for a place like Cumbernauld to boast two or three psycho bands was pretty dramatic. If this was going on in these two unremarkable towns what was happening up and down the country? At the time there was a genuine feeling that Psychobilly, and a whole alternative movement in general, was kicking off like Punk did in 1976/77. This was our thing, totally new, and the cynics could smirk all they fucking wanted to with their accusations that this was just a desperate retread of Rockabilly and Punk. Psychobilly was taking its grip all across the towns and cities of Britain and anyone averse to quiffs, flat-tops and mental music would just have to get used to it.

Psycho-fashion rarely went beyond the traditional T-shirt & denims combo in the early days. L-R: Kenny Mitchell (Termites), Murray (Rednecks), Easterhouse Ian and below Yoker Ian (Salem Dragsters).

Glasgow Psychobilly old-timers and friends, somewhere in Manchester - late 1980's. L-R: John, Pat the Hat, Mish, Balgragon Brian, Murray, (?), Shep & Yoker Ian.

As Kilsyth's anarchy nights had ended so abruptly the prospects of weekends spent in Cumbernauld seemed unthinkable. All they offered were a corner of the pub with my musically like-minded amigos, amongst the local squares and casuals, to a backdrop of pap chart music. Bearing in mind that in those days the charts never boasted the alternative influence it enjoys today. Back then only the shitiest mainstream pop made the Top 40. The most you could ever hope for was a rare spin of some Stray Cats disc. The Cumbernauld psycho-scene had reached capacity and my smalltown boozing days were over. Along with Raymie and Stix, my new Kilsyth mates The Black Puma, Tripney and Bert and a couple of their (even more bumpkin) pals Steven Kelly and Jaggy we got dressed down and made our way into the big smoke.

When the Psychobilly boom really hit Glasgow there was one place you had to be. In the early Eighties, Strutz was No Mean City's stomping mecca. Nestled under the main stage of the world famous Barrowland Ballroom, it was essentially an L-shaped warehouse with a tiny bar, very few seats and almost all of its original 1930's fittings, faded but intact. Obviously whoever first began hosting psycho nights there reasoned that if you dimmed the lights, served the booze and played non-stop 'billy and trash, no one would realise that the place resembled a blitz damaged shell.

Quite simply, no one gave a fuck about the decor as it was a jam-packed punter attraction for the growing number of devotees to this vibrant new movement. Every Friday night the floor shook, the blood spilled and the air was alive with the honk of beer and hairspray. My memories of the place are unsurprisingly blurred but I clearly remember my first night at the club.

After we passed the grumbling, scar-faced bouncers at the small door secreted from the main entrance we made our way through the long, mirror lined corridor which led into the main hall. This provided an ideal opportunity for a last minute quiff check and as we walked along the stomping sounds grew louder. I still recall that as I walked into the hall I was initially overwhelmed by the sheer number of psychobillies and psychobetties. The place was stacked with quiffs, flat-tops, crepes, tartan shirts, cut-off T's, denim, leather and boots, boots, boots! Psychos everywhere, sitting, drinking, dancing, laughing and generally fannying about. The scene was in its early boom and everyone was on board. I was not alone. There were a few odd glares and expressions of bravado sent our way as this was our first appearance but generally the place buzzed with a shared excitement.

During one of our earliest visits to Strutz, my mates and I met up with three girls who were to become a major part of our formative psycho years. Now at this point 'Mills & Boon' romance-ophobes can relax! Its not what you think. Quentin, Tracy and Lorna were around our age and also relative newcomers to the blossoming psycho scene. Quentin was a youthful Queen psychobetty and Trace and Lorna were kind of beat girl/alternative types. After the frosty reception we received from the Glasgow growlers it was nice to see some friendly faces, and after meeting them at the club for a few weeks in a row we eventually accompanied them on most of our nights out in town. Being a trio of attractive young things they often gathered geezers like flies round three pots of sweet honey and, as they introduced us as their mates, we soon got to know a lot of the Glasgow crew, in particular the Easterhouse division. Pat the Hat, Moorsy, Kev the Gerbil, Brian and Big Ian were themselves something of an outsider group like us, stranded on the outskirts of the city in (what was) one of Scotland's most notorious housing schemes. They soon became close friends and also suggested we visit a couple of other psycho-friendly venues such as Vamps and Strathclyde University Students Union.

While Friday nights at Strutz were set in stone, options for Saturday were open. Vamps was a place I never really took to. It was a touch more Goth orientated but played a mix of alternative sounds unlike Strutz more puritan stomping playlist. It also seemed to attract a good number of disgruntled scooterists, mainly ex-mods and skins with some bee in their bonnet over the booming psycho scene. Add to this the huge amount of amyl nitrate sniffed in the bogs and you had an unsettled atmosphere which often erupted into violence.

In addition, the venue was above another club, Vivas, which catered for a heavy casual/chart music loving crowd. Often guerrilla attacks would occur as groups of punters from upstairs would crash into the downstairs club for a quick barney then return to their own part of the venue - or vice versa. The club's owners staggered the closing times to avoid pouring both sets of punters onto the street at the same time but this made little difference, and between 2-3am in Glasgow's Union Street psychobillies and neds could often be found airing their different opinions with fists, boots and bottles.

The other option for Saturday nights, and one that would quickly become a favourite, was Strathclyde University's Student Union (Strathclyde Uni). The Uni was a cavernous venue, eight floors high and stacked with a variety of bars. The Psychobilly haunt was usually the top floor, a massive hall which doubled as a live music venue and boasted a sizable stage. The majority of bands which I witnessed there were pish (remember Eighties big-hair freaks King) but The Milkshakes, King Kurt and Spear of Destiny made rare appearances and I did enter the hall once for an allnighter and was stunned to find the mighty Tall Boys playing unannounced and already half-way through their set. I was mightily pissed off to find that I had been drinking in a downstairs bar with the rest of the Glasgow psychos while Nigel Lewis and the boys bashed out their glorious garage noise to half a room of uninterested students.

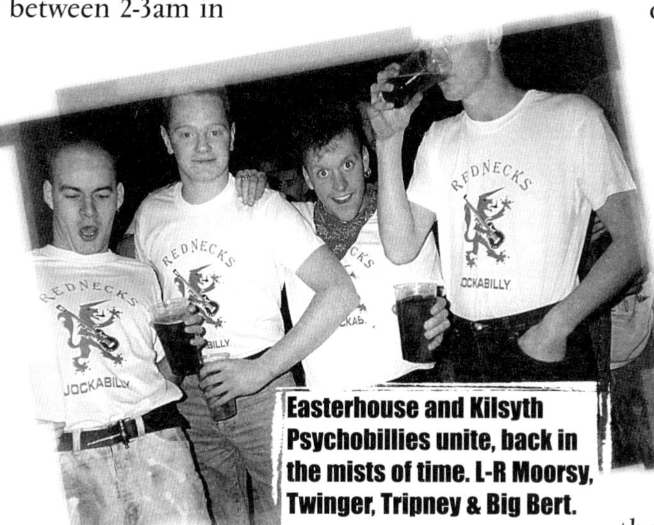

Easterhouse and Kilsyth Psychobillies unite, back in the mists of time. L-R Moorsy, Twinger, Tripney & Big Bert.

For a nightclub, Strathclyde Uni was surprisingly well lit but this only added to its attraction for as soon as you entered the room you could spot the huge number of quiffs hanging together down one whole side of the dancefloor. It was also good for girl-spotting, as the majority of Glasgow's psychobetties chose the Uni to shake their stuff and many a rockin' romance began there including some that are still going strong today.

The top floor played the usual mix of pop pap, golden oldies and joke records usually associated with student discos but they also mixed in enough Ska, Punk and Psychobilly to keep us happy. However, the Uni also boasted another venue within its towering walls which offered the Glasgow crew a fine mix of music in the most spartan of surroundings (ideal for rowdy behaviour and beer spilling).

The dining hall disco was just that, a daytime nosh-up room for students which at night closed the serving hatches and turned the lights (almost) off. It was a sea of formica tables and plastic chairs which were shoved against the walls to make way for merriment. This room regularly rocked to a mix of Ska and Punk alongside a soundtrack of Psychobilly, Trash and 60's Garage Punk. It was here that I received my first schooling in the joys of The Sonics, The Count Five and a whole host of other bands who littered the 'Nuggets' and 'Pebbles' compilation albums (some of the finest collections ever released). They also pushed the garage vibe to its logical conclusion with tracks from The Velvet Underground, MC5 and The Stooges. All in, it drew a good crowd of garage freaks, goths, psychos, skins, punks and even many of Glasgow's large shoe-gazing community (a distant cousin of Lo-Fi and Belle & Sebastian type chimings) and generally everybody mixed well.

Any rumbles that did go down often occurred with lone casuals making a mistaken visit to the venue or student rugby types

The Black Puma enjoys the splendour of the Strathclyde Uni bogs. Late 1980's

attempting to get boisterous. I clearly remember on occasion when a couple of rockabilly kats in our company pummelled one geezer, who had been verbally abusing one of our fine Psychobilly ladies, then immediately tidied up the surrounding tables and chairs leaving the bouncers to find the victim looking as if he had slipped from his stool particularly badly (well, accidents 'can' happen).

The bouncers rarely gave us any grief as, despite resembling a group of boxers approaching retirement, they could distinguish between a bit of rough 'n' tumble and a vicious assault. I only saw them lose the rag once when, after ejecting one of my closest mates (who shall remain nameless) and I, my amigo told the head bouncer calmly and clearly, 'You suck cock!'. The geezer, although well used to standard abuse ('fuck off', 'ya cunt' 'ya fat bastard' etc.) flew into a rage and almost popped a blood vessel. It obviously touched a sore point (oo-er!).

The only small down point about this central hub of Glasgow Psychobilly life was the relentless need to be 'signed in' by bona fide students. As very few of us were partaking in further education, we had to stop students in the street (in those days you could spot them a mile off) and ask if we could be their 'guests'. This usually took the form of applying mild menace to coerce them into getting you in or by adopting a nice-guy Eddie stance and charming them - at least until they got you through the door. This whole process regularly involved crowds of psychobillies badgering the public until one by one they got in, then gave you the finger as they sneaked through the main doors towards warmth, music and beer while you froze your ass off outside like a fucking leper. Being one of the last in felt like being the worst player in a school football team and although you almost always managed to get in it was still a pain-in-the-arse way to start a night of rockin'.

The trouble was that many students were not keen to put their name against a 'billy in the union's guestbook because if you caused a rumpus, by default, they took a share of the blame. Generally though, it was a dopey system as we always got in anyway and if we caused a riot we could be signed in by some other punter the following week. The Black Puma finally put the whole need to dick about to rest anyway when he got a job in a printers and made us a stack of bogus ID cards. Obviously at this time in the mid-Eighties, Glasgow had plenty to offer a Psychobilly looking for action on a Friday and Saturday night... and for anytime in between their was always Hurricanes.

Hurricanes was a very small bar stashed in the basement of a victorian-type office block. It lay within Glasgow's office district and, although it was only minutes away from the heart of the city, it was always a deadly quiet area outside normal working hours (apart from inside of course). As you walked along the street a small sign flashed at knee height, and you then descended down a short flight of steps. How, or when, Hurricanes became a mecca for Glasgow's alternative types I do not know but my mates and I discovered it very soon after our first trip to Strutz and after that first visit I spent almost every Thursday to Saturday night there until it closed its doors.

For me, it was the first place that I ever felt a 'regular', the atmosphere was always buzzing and good-natured and I met many punters within those walls who are still mates today. Although it was tiny - low ceiling, about eight tables and two piss-pots - it attracted most of Glasgow's alternative types at one time or another. Punks, goths, skins and psychobillies mingled together in these cramped conditions while posers were sent down the road to 'The Rock Garden', home of bequiffed nancy boys like Hipsway, Love & Money and The Bluebells.

Unusually, the bar owners never actively pitched the pub at an alternative audience and rarely played any suitable sounds but most folks were only there for the booze and a chance to chat to their mates before hitting the nightclubs, where dancing and shouting were the only options. Most nights almost everyone knew each other, a rare treat in Glasgow's city centre which normally featured bars full of strangers from across the region. Hurricane's was the essential warm-up to a full night on the town and weekend boozing started around lunchtime on Friday (after a Thursday night warm-up) until closing time Sunday night, so there was rarely an hour in which you could not indulge in the Glasgow psycho-scene.

While this book was never intended to document the history of Psychobilly music (even though it is a good idea), I do feel it would be farcical not to at least mention a few of the scene's seminal albums which, I feel, are a host of debut offerings and a fistful of ground-breaking compilation LP's.

Face up to it... mainstream Eighties music was shite. Every time I see one of these TV advertised collections of Eighties pop hits I want to wipe my arse on the screen. I break into a cold sweat when I realise that processed, electro-pop pap could have been the soundtrack to my life if I had not been saved by a higher power. I was on a one-way ticket to being just like every other eighties square, streaking my hair, wearing pastel-coloured Miami Vice clobber and listening to mindless chart music. But I was saved brothers & sisters, saved (hallelujah), saved (gather your limbs) by that mystical, musical monster they called the Psychobilly and Trash revolution.

Thankfully, a new breed of Psychobilly bands created a rash of vinyl releases that shone like diamonds amongst the pile of shite that was Eighties mainstream music and with the benefit of hindsight (or if you are an old fuck like me) it is important to remember just how important many of these early releases were. Many of Psychobilly's landmark releases were outstanding debuts or pioneering compilation & live albums, and none kicked off a musical genre in greater style than The Meteors 1981 debut 'In Heaven'.

I do not know if it is even worth mentioning specific tracks on 'In Heaven' as they are all genuinely true classics. Everyone must admit that even the finest albums often conceal a few weak tracks but this LP is a rarity... all killers, no fillers! From start to finish this album turned a whole generation on to Psychobilly. No matter when you dived into the psycho lifestyle, without 'In Heaven' there would have been nothing.

This album provided a welcome alternative to thousands of punters who were bored stiff with the shitty state of music in the early Eighties. If you have any interest in rockin' music and you have not heard this album... sort yourself out! Now that Psychobilly has drifted off in many different and extreme directions, many folks might have forgotten the impact this album made but when it was released there was simply nothing like it.

Although reams of great bands and shelf-loads of fine albums were to follow in the Psychobilly tsunami this release created, it firmly established The Meteors as the Godfathers of Psychobilly and why the fuck it took seventeen years for this album to make it onto CD is beyond me. I got into The Meteors debut album around the start of 1983, so by this time further treats were just around the corner including another album that would truly define the Psychobilly movement 'Wreckin Crew'. After some extensive personnel shuffling, P. Paul Fenech further staked his claim on Psychobilly's creation with this amazing album that delivered a real kick in the pants and thrust this new genre further into your face with a barrel-load of tunes which are icons of all that is psycho (and billy).

Then like an incoming bazooka, King Kurt splurged onto the scene with 'Ooh Wallah Wallah', their 1983 debut LP that sounded like the bastard son of Rockabilly, Punk, Rock 'n' Roll, Glam Rock, Bo Diddley & Benny Hill. As a youthful Psychobilly, just recovering from a double-whammy of excellent Meteors albums, I felt King Kurt took their brand of Psychobilly off in a totally different direction.

In retrospect, this album hinted at the (temporary) belief that the music biz had in Psychobilly as the 'next big thing'. 'Ooh Wallah Wallah' was produced by Dave Edmunds, a well respected rock 'n' roller who had already produced The Stray Cats and had many hits of his own over three decades, and it was released by Stiff Records, a legendary label which had helped pioneer Pub Rock, Punk, New Wave and even Two-Tone in the UK. The album was also backed up with some major promotion in the form of gigs, press publicity and even some entertaining promos. Yet again there is no point in mentioning specific tracks (I'm sure you all know them) as this album is a solid-gold legend in the psycho-strato-sphere.

What was most exciting at the time was the amount of variety on offer as each new debut album added yet another new flavour to Psychobilly. From the shadow of Neo-Rockabilly legends The Sharks came Frenzy, driving Rockabilly straight into Psychobilly in a bass-slapping blur and delivering excellent tunes such as 'I See Red' and 'Nobody's Business' which still remain psycho classics. Restless were also blurring the edges of the Psychobilly scene and, while still remaining resolutely Rockabilly, they had a hard and fast sound that I feel attracted a larger share of psycho followers than many purist Rockabilly bands.

I am not a great fan of live albums as they are often rushed out by record companies to fill a gap between a band's studio albums or a tatty collection of poorly recorded groups. But when you have The Milkshakes, Restless, The Sting-Rays and The Guana Batz on top form live at Psychobilly's London headquarters you cannot fail... and 'Stomping at the Klub Foot: Vol 1' doesn't. Its a stone-cold classic piece of psycho-trash history. Four bands, four tracks each and a real snapshot of the excitement and vitality of the new Psychobilly and Trash boom. Not only did this album kick off a whole series of Klub Foot releases but it also established the venue's name as a, still memorable, Psychobilly mecca of the Eighties and a place as fondly remembered by aging psychos as the Wigan Casino is by floor-bothering Northern Soul devotees.

I'm pretty sure that when 'Hell's Bent on Rockin' first appeared it was slightly overshadowed in the compilation market by the likes of 'Stomping at the Klub Foot' and 'Blood on the Cats'. Whether this was the case or not, it is still an important chunk of vinyl which deserves a place in psycho-history as many of the tracks, to this day, can still leave you in a rockin' frenzy. Despite a couple of weak moments from bands / singers who shall remain nameless (you know who I mean) the album is packed full of wreckin' goodness. First off it boasts a couple of early Demented Are Go tracks, 'Rubber Rock' and 'One Sharp Knife'. These tunes were a pre-debut album taster of the perverted goodness that was to follow and totally essential. The mighty Steve Whitehouse also makes a double appearance, first off with The Sharks classic 'Ghost Train' then a very early version of 'Cry or Die' by Frenzy. Rounding the whole lot off are Tracks from The Meteors, The Deltas, The Rapids, The Outer Limits, The Richocets and those occasionally pyjama-clad rockers, Restless. Yet again another album slightly out of focus in the mists of time but still a whacked-out collection of what was happening on the psycho and Neo-Rockabilly scene.

By 1985 many psycho's were scratching their heads wondering

just what the fuck had happened to the debut LP which The Guana Batz had referred to on the first 'Stomping at the Klub Foot' album. The band were driving the punters mental at gigs all over the country but only a single, The Cave, was available to the record buying public. What was going on. Half way through the year and still no sign of anything. Could The Batz not get a record deal? (unlikely). Were they just taking the time to get it right? (probably). Whatever the story... it was worth the wait.

The aptly named 'Held Down To Vinyl... At Last' eventually appeared and, surprisingly, for a debut Psychobilly LP it kicked off with a (relatively) mellow track. 'Down on the Line' is a catchy tune with a busking feel and apart from 'Can't Take The Pressure', Side One boasts a relaxed set of tunes which was unique in a time when many fledgling psycho bands saw faster songs as the way forward. But speed freaks did not have to worry as Side Two started with the mental pace of the classic 'King Rat' and steamrolled its way to the end, only pausing for breath with 'Please Give Me Something'. This was a long-awaited debut of great originality which was much more than the flat out stompfest many expected and it confirmed The Batz as one of the legends of UK Psychobilly.

As the Psychobilly scene really began to establish itself on vinyl, speeding over the horizon came two other groundbreaking debuts from Torment and Demented Are Go which pushed the genre onto new heights of composition and further depths of depravity. I had seen and heard little of Torment when I bought a copy of their debut platter in 1986. 'Psyclops Carnival' seemed a bizarre title and it looked a little different to many of the psycho albums released up to that point, with its stark black & white imagery and sombre tone. After giving it a first spin I was initially unimpressed as it lacked a certain boot-stomping immediacy but as I continued to play it the tracks really grew on me. Like many of the songs on The Guana Batz debut, there were many lyrics expressing personal concerns and steadfastly avoiding what were then psycho-standard themes such as horror, graveyards, getting pissed and mental patients. While I do not intend to get all chin-strokingly philosophical here, it can not be denied that Torment offered another level of intelligent songwriting, mostly from the pen of

Simon Brand, along with yet another radical reworking of the traditional twangy geetar, drums and double-bass line-up.

It was only a few years ago that I discovered while thumbing through a copy of Deathrow Database fanzine that Torment's lead singer, Simon Brand, had killed himself. It was a bit of a shock even though I had not heard anything of the band for ages. I met Simon only once, in the khazi of a pub near the Bierkeller in Bristol, the venue for one of the many 'Night of the Long Knives' gigs. We talked briefly and he seemed a pleasant geezer but I mumbled a bit as I was always a big fan of the band and got a bit star struck.

Torment were one of the many excellent Psychobilly bands which I felt could have had major success had they continued, weathered the quiet years, and been offered the opportunity to cash in on the type of big-time record deals offered to many Yank and Aussie bands since the late Nineties. They really stuck out on the UK psycho scene with a distinct image, well crafted songs with strong lyrical content and a really unique sound.

In the same year, kicking open the doors to a new breed of psycho-perverts everywhere was the stunning debut from Demented Are Go, 'In Sickness & In Health'. This album starts off with a mind-bending version of 'Be Bop A Lula' and follows classic track with classic track right to the end. This album contains absolutely NO weak tracks and, again, it sent Psychobilly off in a totally new direction. First off singer, and soon to be psycho-legend, Mark Phillips appeared on the cover in make-up and a dress. This might be old hat now but at the time few people could work out what the fuck this band were all about. With their onstage props of dildos and blow-up sex dolls and a peek at their early songs: 'Rubber Buccaneer', 'Rubber Love', 'Pervy in the Park' & 'PVC Chair', you soon got the hint of the perversion that was to follow.

As well as the unique high-pervo content, 'In Sickness..' also boasts a heap of tracks which instantly became Psychobilly classics. Who could ever forget 'Transvestite Blues', Holy Hack Jack', 'Vibrate' and their total mangling of that old Osmonds track 'Crazy Horses'. It is hard to imagine that this album is over seventeen years old as it still has the power to drive you mental!

From the mid-Eighties onwards, almost every month new debut albums continued to appear with very few regurgitating or aping other bands. It was still open doors at the Psychobilly saloon and, as demand was growing, labels such as Nervous, ID, Raucous, Fury, Link & Anagram kept 'em coming. Lost Moment was another label who unleashed a cracking Psychobilly debut, The Krewmen's 'Adventures of the Krewmen'. This was an excellent album, very well produced and with great cover art which left you in know doubt as to the band's influences and direction. I may be mistaken but I got the impression that The Krewmen were the 'lone gunslingers' of the psycho-scene at that time as they did not seem to appear on the same amount of compilations or play the same venues with the regularity of many other Eighties Psychobilly pioneers. Though plagued by line-up changes as their career progressed, I still do not think that The Krewmen get the respect they deserve for playing their part in the early psycho-scene. They knocked out a heap of foot-stomping classics and memorable cover versions and their fine back catalogue of albums simply proves my point.

Another firm favourite of mine was Skitzo's first vinyl outing 'Skitzo Mania'. Yet another variation on the psycho-theme, a solid sprint through the key elements of Psychobilly and a rough 'n' rapid style that hinted at the future direction of these Psychobilly speed-freaks. This is an album which suited to an evening snorting snakebite and Red Bull and their stylish reworking of 'Lonesome Train' outdoes even King Kurt's version.

Cattle-prodding their way into the scene from a completely different angle were The Long Tall Texans. This relentlessly cheerful trio dared to introduce melody, catchy songwriting and glossy production onto their albums and quickly became favourites amongst legions of UK 'billies. The Texans probably did more than most to bring psycho to a wider audience and as a live act they were immensely popular with their combination of foot-shuffling tracks and all out wrecking pit shakers. They really knew how to work a crowd and were probably one of the tightest live acts around. They also boasted the infamy of being captured by an arty photographer who made prints of the band available in Athena shops up and down the country alongside other iconic images such as 'musclebound poseur holding a baby' and 'tennis bird scratching her arse'.

Another debut treat on offer

was 'Ein Bier Bitte' from The Coffin Nails. I always liked The coffin Nails as they dished out fine entertainment and did not seem to take themselves too seriously. I once saw them perform live almost a full set of their songs in a 'disco-billy' style. Half of the po-faced punters in the audience did not get it but at least they had the bollocks to try it. 'Ein Bier Bitte' was their debut platter and an often ignored Eighties psycho classic. Although it sounds as if it was rattled out in a few days studio time nearly every track is memorable, not least their crowd-pleasing anthem 'Let's Wreck'. The album also contains the country hoedown / bumpkin' fuckin' gem 'Uncle Willy', a sleazy sex track 'Penetration', the fucking outrageous 'Myra Hindley' and an instrumental named after the band's big-bellied guitarist 'Humungus'. The Coffin Nails' six string king eventually took over lead vocals as well, after another line-up reshuffle, and they have constantly kept recording and playing live to this day. They remain a class bunch of psycho-survivors who never seemed to get the attention they deserved.

Finally, pushing the psycho-lifestyle to its extremes were The Frantic Flintstones. Their debut album 'Nightmare on Nervous' set a new template for excellent slap-bass led Psychobilly focusing on drugs, booze and general depravity. Driven by main man Chuck Flintstone, they seemed to record, play live and get wrecked almost consistently and the trail they blazed from the early Eighties until now has scorched itself across the face of UK Psychobilly. They also had a healthy disregard for any unwritten laws of Psychobilly and their use of gospel, country and a whole heap of other musical styles may be common now but was groundbreaking back in 'ye olden dayes'.

Although these are but a few of the fine bands who broke onto the Eighties psycho-scene, they all proved how vibrant and varied Psychobilly was and this was only from the bands willing to accept the Psychobilly monicker. Way down south another new genre was opening to all lovers of demented rock 'n' roll and, although many of these bands actively attempted to distance themselves from the Psychobilly brand, a new beat explosion had burst its way from the trashcans and was forcing its way beyond the garage door.

Where's all the Psychobilly bands? Whoops! Wrong festival.
L-R: Raymie, Big Bert & Bracko at Glastonbury 1986.

Bracko & The Black Puma's attempt to hitch a train ride to Hemsby was a complete waste of time.

Chapter 5:
These cats ain't nuthin but...

Alongside the straight ahead Psychobilly boom another, more London-centric, offshoot caught my attention in a big way. The Trash scene featured a selection of bands who blended a variety of different genres such as Punk, R&B, British Beat, Psychedelia, Rockabilly, Sixties Garage and a myriad of other underground sounds. What it all boiled down to was excitement and pure adrenalin driven Rock 'n' Roll.

At the forefront of this scene was undoubtably Thee Milkshakes. Though Thee Milkshakes head man, Billy Childish, would probably poke his own eye out with a paintbrush rather than be attributed as the leading light of any movement, with an almost incalculable back catalogue it cannot be denied that he pioneered a punk-influenced, back-to-basics, rockin' racket, from his earliest days in The Pop Rivets, through Thee Milkshakes and beyond with Thee Mighty Ceasars, Thee Headcoats and his present creation The Buff Medway. I caught most of these bands through the years and always admired their rugged sound, constant abusement of the audience and refusal to use modern PA's in favour of authentic valve-driven amps.

A band which I never caught live, to my great teeth-knashing despair, were The Cannibals. Much like Thee Milkshakes, The Cannibals were a loosely altering line-up which centred on garage punk fanatic, exiled yank, Mike Spenser. The Cannibals defied definition as they threw surf instrumentals, freakbeat, deep psychedelia and a whole lot of other shit into a missionary-boiling pot. Only in recent years, after viewing a late-night documentary on British TV, did I realise that Spenser had arrived in the UK with a fine pedigree in the American Punk / New Wave scene of the Seventies. Whatever his credentials, The Cannibals were excellent purveyors of garage goodness and effectively defined 'Trash' itself. I even read a bizarre article at the time in which Spenser was attempting to badger supremos at Woolworths into stocking a selection of Trash albums in every store. Cannibals albums amongst the pick 'n' mix? Fan-fucking-tastic!

As if to further enhance the growing reputation of trash, 'The Tube' (at that time Britain's only quality music programme on TV) treated the nation to 'Four On Four - Trash on the Tube', one Friday night in 1984. This was the finest television I had witnessed since King Kurt's TOTP appearance, made even more special by the fact that rockin' music was rarely featured on the box while pop pap and boring pomp was in plentiful supply.

Thee Milkshakes, The Sting-Rays, Tall Boys & The Prisoners performed a track each at an invite-only gig in front of the movers & shakers of the London trash 'n' psycho scene. Thee Milshakes kicked it off with Out of Control, closely followed by The Prisoners (in full 60's Star Trek clobber) with Reaching My Head. Then The Sting- Rays proved their live prominence with an unforgettable blast through Come On Kid and Tall Boys wrapped it up with a driving rendition of Ride This Torpedo. It was a quality film, perfectly capturing the excitement and variety of the Trash scene and its subsequent release as an E.P. was, I feel, the seven-inch event of the Eighties. This was also another defining moment for me as a youthful psycho as it offered further confirmation that this underground music movement was thundering ahead into the mainstream and only a half-wit would dare miss a moment of the rockin' good times ahead.

Seeing 'Trash on the Tube', much like witnessing King Kurt's appearance on TOTP, was another major revelation to me probably because it gave real legitimacy to the growing grip that Psychobilly and Trash were exerting on the nation. It also gave me my first 'live' peek at a band who were, and still remain, one of my firm favourites from that era. The Sting-Rays were an enigma. Initially exploding onto the scene with assorted quiffs and a slap-bass, they were unlike any other bands associated with this image. Like many Trash bands of the time they seemed to have a sometimes uneasy relationship with their Psychobilly following and during their stint as main support on a Cramps tour they claimed onstage "Psychobilly is dead". Obviously an overstatement but this perhaps led from their fear of being branded a specific type of music. However, The Sting-Rays were impossible to categorise anyway and a unique blend of 60's Garage Punk, Rockabilly, Beat and Psychedelia is the nearest definition I can find. What they offered (on vinyl and onstage) is far easier to name... pure excitement.

I tracked down the band's debut album 'Dinosaurs', an LP which is hard to describe as each song has its own style and generally this debut does not immediately register on the old grey matter but with repeated listening it offers plentiful rewards. They seemed to be a band who were unafraid to explore another dimension in the studio rather than simply laying down their live set in a workmanlike fashion. This sits rather unusually alongside their furious, chaotic and frantic live energy perfectly captured on 'Trash on the Tube', their live album 'Live Retaliation' and their quartet of tracks on the first 'Stomping at the Klub Foot' album. Despite their disdain for Psychobilly, I continued to enjoy The Sting- Rays as their sound progressed wildly and I still feel that they were one of the most innovative bands to emerge from the Trash boom. On the release of their first compilation CD, which appeared on Big Beat in 2002, I damn near wet the bed with excitement as it perfectly captures their wild and varied career.

Another two bands from the Trash scene that knocked me sideways were Tall Boys and The Vibes. As The Meteors bass player and joint frontman during their earliest incarnation, Nigel Lewis was already an almost legendary figure in the Psychobilly stratosphere. After dabbling, along with P. Paul Fenech, as The Clapham South Escalators his next band Tall Boys strayed further from the Psychobilly template with their own rumbling, menacing sound. Featuring fellow ex-Meteor Mark Robertson on drums and joined by guitarist James Alan, and occasional bassist Kevin Green, they produced a scattering of releases, including their LP 'Wednesday Adams' Boyfriend' and the fantastic 12" 'Final Kick'. Each release made the band's sound no easier to categorise but cemented their position as solid innovators of the Trash scene. Further on in his career, Lewis released a quirky solo album in 1986 'What I Feel Now ' then appeared to go undercover until reappearing in the mid-Nineties with The Johnson Family.

A question that has consistently bugged me since the sweet sound of Trash seeped from beneath the garage door was who were The Vibes? They skirted around the Trash scene, pumped out a couple of singles, an album, appeared on 'John Peel's Festive Fifty', became The Purple Things and (after a few excellent mini-LP's)... disappeared! In that short time they left behind some of the most excellent British Trash tracks ever and still remain an enigma.

Their album 'What's Inside'

was a psycho-delic experience, and their 12" 'Inner Wardrobes Of Your Mind' was an acid-fried brain melter, but they kicked the whole thing off with an excellent four-track EP 'Can You Feel...' that combined a menacing stomp, garage-punk, go-go and even a touch of mambo. All their releases boasted a knockout combination of key trash influences and a healthy slap-bass. I never caught them live and could find little about them other than that their double-bass player also was a member of The Blubbery Hellbellies and (I think) The Sting- Rays and some of them came from Liverpool. Whatever their story, they produced some of the finest tracks known to Trash and even Radio One's baldy, beardy indie god agreed.

While these are but a few of the bands who contributed to the Trash genre, it has to be said that they were all far too good to be limited to the confines of any vague 'scene' and as such they soon progressed onwards in a variety of directions. No doubt this was inevitable as it was the wide range of influences which the groups drew from which made the Trash flame burn so brightly (and so quickly). Furthermore, no matter if I was to work my fingers to bloody stumps attempting to define Trash, two classic compilation albums: 'These Cats Ain't Nothin But Trash' and 'Rockabilly Psychosis and The Garage Disease' say far more about this rag-bag of Rock 'n' Roll geniuses than I ever could. Keeping in mind an excellent surf & instrumental scene, which had close links to a number of Trash bands and venues, and in retrospect the mid-Eighties had a lot to offer the seeker of rockin' rythmns despite often being perceived as a barren period of New Romantic nonsense and pop pap.

While much of UK psycho-history has been written south of the border and in Europe, Scotland has made some contribution over the decades. One of the few Scottish trash bands who played regularly across Jockoland at the scene's beginnings were The Styng-Rites. I never found out whether their oddly spelt name came about for specific reasons or because they were beaten to the punch by Crouch End's finest The Sting-Rays (themselves no doubt employing a hyphen to avoid legal action from puppet-puller Gerry Anderson). Regardless of that they were, in my opinion, Scotland's finest rockin' export since The Poets. As they were deemed suitable for inclusion on one of the seminal 'Klub Foot' live albums I can only imagine others shared my belief.

The Styng-Rites were a furiously entertaining, good-time band with a unique spaceabilly image and a Vox cabinet full of great tunes. Rather than sticking rigidly to the Psychobilly template they seemed to boast a range of influences, most notably The Revillos/Rezillos but also British Beat, Screaming Lord Sutch and trad Rock 'n' Roll. However, like their namesakes down south they appeared to feel restricted by the Psychobilly scene.

It seemed to me that they began to feel pigeonholed by the psycho tag and grew tired of much of their relentlessly rowdy followers. But it was quite simply impossible not to go mental to their stack of great tunes such as 'Reptile Man', 'Dogfish' and their high-octane version of Sutch's 'Murder In The Graveyard'. It was not to be the first time that a rockin' Eighties band would look down, with a purist attitude, on Psychobilly - a bastard mix of music genres (but we love it).

Regardless of that, they began to pursue a more rockin' pop vibe which had an adverse effect. They became too pop for the Psychobilly audience while punters, who perhaps would have appreciated their new direction, assumed their gigs were for knuckleheads only. Eventually they disbanded but George Millar, the lead singer, appeared once again in the Nineties fronting the immaculately authentic British Beat barons The Kaisers.

The Radium Cats were another accomplished Scot's rock 'n' roll outfit who, while happy to play to Psychobilly punters, often stressed their influences from the Fifties, B-movies, voodoo and the culture of The Cramps. I saw them play on many occasions and always enjoyed their super tight three-piece style of guitar, slap-bass and snare. They were most probably also Jockland's most prestigious group in terms of record releases with some cracking stuff on Raucous Records and a scattering of other recordings.

Bizarrely, as they hailed from Edinburgh, I know little else from the band as a mysterious divide seems to exist between Glasgow and the capital. Despite being only forty miles apart, both cities are extremely different and culturally ruptured. We would often travel to London to see a band rather than nip across to Edinburgh.

Away from the central belt, Aberdeen also boasted a lively psycho-scene which gave many of the top psycho bands on tour a chance to receive a warm Northern welcome. The Numbskulls were the 'Deen's greatest export and their bass player Strangy eventually moved to the big smoke to join The Klingonz and latterly Celtic Bones. Other members of the band still play to this very day in Aberdeen Rock 'n' Roll band King Voodoo along with ex-Glasgow rocker Rod Vegas.

Further south in Kilmarnock, almost 'Wicker man' territory, seeped the sound of one of Jockland's most authentic Psychobilly voices - The Termites. Kenny, Bally, Gerry & Ewin first came to national prominence with their self-titled E.P. on Raucous Records followed by their excellent debut album 'Overload' on Link in 1990. The back cover of 'Overload' featured a photo-montage, that classic staple of Psychobilly-influenced cover design, which is a perfect example of Glasgow's psycho-scene at that time. The album was also a perfect example of The Termites hardcore Psychobilly style and despite a splattering of appearances on a number of compilations, a second album never materialised.

With a bit more studio cash behind them The Termites could easily have improved on 'Overload' and continued to release memorable Psychobilly albums but it (for whatever reasons) was not to be. I saw the band many times and they always provided solid entertainment. There is no doubt that they spread the word on Scottish Psychobilly across the UK and Europe and even the most po-faced rocker would surely find it hard to remain un-rocked by their blistering live performances and rare vinyl outings. 'Fuck All night', indeed!

I am sure that there are a few other Jockabilly bands I am unable to mention through ignorance and hazy memory particles and also a few I know little about such as The Full Moon Freaks (who make a brief appearance on Raucous Records' 'Psycho Tendencies' compilation) and The Primevals (a heavy garage act from Greenock who appeared on the second 'Stomping At The Klub Foot' album). That is not to say that us jocks did without as Scotland was a regular pit-stop for touring psycho bands and it has consistently had a quality Rockabilly scene, with bands such as The Cottonfield Boys and The Razorcuts, and a fantastic selection of authentic Garage Punk bands like The Green Telescope and The Beeville Hive Five, mostly playing around Edinburgh. And anyway, heaps of live 'billy could be found by attempting yet another motorway journey over the border, in the back of a van with a pile of other smelly bastards.

The long, short & medium quiff... just three of the exciting options open to your Psychobilly barber. L-R: Brian, Moorsy, Murray & Jane.

Old-school Psycho-style: Flat-top, sleeveless T-shirt, bleached denims & can of lager (optional). Burty - Night of the Long Knives, Birmingham.

The image of Psychobilly was always going to be one associated (rightly or wrongly) with violence and a certain amount of boneheaded activity. Shaved heads, tattoos, ripped denim, boots and leather have always carried an essence of menace which was undeniably part of the attraction of that style. These days, clobber of that kind is almost completely mainstream, fourteen-up boots and Motorhead T-shirts are now available in Top Man (for fuck's sake) but in the Eighties the Psychobilly image was mucho alternative.

As well as the standard psycho uniform of jeans, t-shirt and tartan shirt there were a few fashionable fads in the early days which seemed to fade as the scene progressed. The most major, and bemusing, of these was the 'ski jumper', an item of clothing that is difficult to explain as each jumper had a whacko, varied design but basically they were crew-neck woollen pullovers with a winter design. The more subtle designs had combinations of snowflakes in various sizes but for the advanced ski-jumper clad rocker options with snowmen, reindeer and Christmas trees were available. Generally, most of these bizarre creations boasted different bands of colour at the waist and neck. Completely out of step with psycho-fashion then and now, I never had one of these but plenty did and for anyone who has never encountered this item of clothing, check out some early snaps of The Sharks or The Guana Batz and you are bound to spot at least one.

Baseball jackets and fringed suede jackets were also regularly worn but often proved a touch more expensive (and less resilient) than the good old biker's leather or pilot jacket. Pilot jackets in particular were useful as the majority of them were olive green and you could occasionally leave a venue with someone else's and end the evening a few bob up or with some extra fags. But woe and betide anyone caught slipping on your meticulously hand-painted biker's jacket as these were often the pride and joy of most psychobillies. My main one had a full 'skull 'n' confederate flag' logo accompanied by a smaller Elvis Hitler 'Hellbilly' banner and a shitey skull on the arm with 'Deathshead' written underneath it so pathetically that it looked like 'Death Shed'. How the kids tittered when my attempts to scrape it off failed.

Continuing with the theme of relatively short-lived items of psycho gear, shorts were heavily in as essential items of gig-going wear right into the Big Rumble days, often accompanied 'only' by white or fluorescent socks. Denim dungarees alsohad a real boom in the late-Eighties, though they still remain a favourite of die-hard hillbillies. And who remembers that Restless-inspired pyjama wearing phase. I do not know if this fad spread through the UK but Glasgow certainly had a lot of psychos out for the weekend dressed in bri-nylon bed gear and boots.

Haircuts were obviously another crucial element of the Psychobilly style that seemed to bemuse, and in some cases panic, joe public. The starting point for many punters on discovering the psycho scene was the short flat-top, a 2-3 inch table top with a number one or two at the sides and back. As the scene progressed the tops began developing a gradient, often from a modest inch at the back to 5-6 inches at the front then eventually from nowt at the back to as much as hairspray could control out front. At the sides it became total all-off with a bare razor and any more than a number one was frowned upon. Other early options included a 'rim' of quiff round the bonce with everything else, including most of the top, shaved off. As the scene progressed almost anything went but early barnets seemed to be relatively uniform, with much blond hair dye splashed on with careless abandon. In my earliest memories it was often easy to tell which punters had been skins or rockabillies before psycho as the skins started to grow a bit on top (and kept the pilot jackets) while the rockabillies kept their quiffs and simply shaved off the back and sides (still sporting their biker leathers and baseball jackets).

I always had great problems with my barnet as baby soft hair and rapidly approaching baldness combined to make my quiff-creating times a mighty pain in the arse. Even with a short flat-top I needed industrial-strength gel and hairspray to create that much desired squarehead look. I favoured a cheapo high-street brand of spray, known as 'Falcon Death Grip', which I battered away with so frequently that I must surely have poked my own hole in the ozone.

Despite the image which many psychobillies fostered in the

Eighties you were almost always more likely to be on the receiving end of a kicking from a casual slacks wearing dickhead in a pastel coloured shirt. Again and again bouncers would turn us away from pubs and clubs to avoid 'trouble' while some tit with a side-shed and a moustache would breeze in then cheerfully set about somebody with a Stanley knife before closing time.

In those early days my folks were wholesale victims of the folk devil propaganda of the time and were terrified that my clobber and haircut would have the neighbours thinking I was a 'skinhead'. How I mocked and jeered their fears as, despite my pilot jacket, Doc Martens, tight jeans and turn-ups, my hair was a good one inch longer on top than your average bovver boy. How on earth could Joe Public ever mistake me for one of my Oi-loving amigos? Now, as an old podger, I tee-hee at how confident I was of my individuality. These days I often categorise every baseball-capped, tracksuit-wearing youth as a junky thug probably packing a blade or a dirty needle.

Despite all that, serious trouble was generally avoided. At Psychobilly gigs and venues most of the pummelling happened on the dance floor and some of the more raucous nights in the wrecking pit made a kicking outside the kebab shop seem the easy option. I also found this theme much the same in the world of hardcore punk and thrash metal moshing. The attitude was 'let those crazy kids punch fuck out of each other on the dancefloor and get it out of their system' and bouncers often spent more time picking up teeth from the floor after closing than scrapping with the punters outside. Besides, any psycho venue worth its salt had bouncers who could tell the difference between a full-bodied stomping sesh and a bar-room brawl (even though they often had a close resemblance).

Out on the streets we often hung around in such large groups that we were rarely bothered by ordinary bams. To me the casuals, neds, plebs (whatever) that I was surrounded by in Cumbernauld and Glasgow were boneheadedly territorial, scrapping with other half-wits from the neighbouring area often only streets away. Housing scheme against housing scheme, town against town, Catholics against protestants... pointless. What I enjoyed about the Psychobilly scene was that I had mates from all over Glasgow, gathered together by a shared enthusiasm. Had things been different for us all we would probably only have glared at each other (or worse) in the city centre and only mixed with geezers from our own part of town. What a waste, fuck that small-minded shit.

In my experience there were also few barneys with other devotees of youth culture. We regularly hung around with skins, goths and rockabillies. Some of the '69 traditional skins, early scooterists and rockabillies were a bit sniffy about Psychobilly (probably because it had plundered the best elements of their style) but, apart from a few scuffles, most of these punters generally got on. After all, we were all part of an alternative movement to the shite music and high-street fashion of the decade and, unlike today, you had to choose a side and stick to it as the mainstream (then) had no place for a lot of weirdoes with short hair and scruffy clobber.

In the late Seventies things had not been so easy going in Glasgow as teds, punks, mods and skins regularly clashed on the city streets. Add to this the city's notorious football related bigotry and Saturdays in the city centre were wild times and I often witnessed extended street battles from afternoon until late in the evening.

Regardless of petty rivalries I was always glad to meet other psychobillies and would often approach other brethren to chat about the psycho scene and most folks, if not openly friendly, would a least be civil and I met a host of new rockin' mates. Before this makes the Psychobilly community sound like a hippy, trippy love cult, it has to be said that not everyone shared my ideals. The early days of Psychobilly in Glasgow were rife with divisions based on territorial lines and a quick trip to places like Paisley, Grangemouth or Aberdeen could guarantee you a warm, welcoming kicking. As my mates and I were regarded as Cumbernauld & Kilsyth psychos (roughly translated as cowshit stained incomers) we were widely disregarded by many of the Glasgow mobs for ages. I was almost on the end of a glassing from one motley crew of East End hoodlums who wound up some half-wit and sent him after me with a broken pint pot. However, not long after we settled our differences and became good mates I discovered that Murray, a close friend and band member, was one of the culprits. How we tee-hee'd at that revelation.

Another incident that brought on more giggles than goingovers happened one weekend at one of London's infamous 'Night of the Long Knives' bonanzas. A large group of us travelled down together in a transit van and being the almost token jocks at this large event we may have attracted some unwelcome attention but that was always part of the game... so fuck it! The atmosphere was heightened as this was around the time of the 'Meteors versus the world' period and many of the Londoners were steadfastly in one camp or the other.

Apart from some usual eyeballing from The Kattle, our only brush with violence came in the shape of our Deutschland brethren. At one point, my mate Pat and I were outside the venue taking a piss / smoking a joint etc, when a tall and po-faced German psycho asked us "Do you want to rumble?". Firstly, after twelve hours cramped in a van with fifteen other sweaty Scotsmen the only thing that was rumbling was my arse. Secondly, who the fuck 'rumbles' anyone other than dopey teens in old 1950's juvenile delinquent films? We burst out laughing, to the geezer's bemusement, turned down his offer in a jovial manner and he stomped of - confused.

As the years progressed, and many fairweather trend followers moved on, many of the divisions in Glasgow disappeared. With the scene becoming smaller we tended to stick together and formed a tighter band of rockin' enthusiasts. With few areas apart from Easterhouse boasting a reasonable number of psychos, Glasgow's Psychobilly collective drew on disparate punters from all over the West of Scotland. For this reason, the Glasgow scene became reasonably jovial with few real barneys amongst the crew and, as we spent so much time hanging together, few intrusions from Joe Soap and his mates. Again, there were certainly a few amongst our psycho brotherhood who could start a fight in an empty house (and shall remain nameless) but few serious interactions went down and any punch-ups were able to be smoothed out after a short while.

Ironically, after years of wrecking, most of my major injuries came from ice-skating accidents, drunken tumbles, ex-girlfriends and the occasional Meteors gig. My main interest was always the music and having a good time and even though the few nights I spent in casualty did not fill me with glee, Psychobilly has always been a full-contact sport and nobody can deny that a bout of wreckin' does have its own unique charm. Something which I ponder fondly as I drop my false tooth into steradent every night.

Four more converts to the mid-1980's scooter scene. Don't know about those shady ETS' though... L-R: The Black Puma, Tripney, Big Bert & Bracko.

.. but back soon on a PX - the classic Vespa. L' bent for leather!

Chapter 8

Two Wheels Burnin' - Discovering the scooter scene.

One weekend in Glasgow our psychobetty amigos Quentin, Tracy and Lorna disappeared to some English seaside resort while we dug in to two nights of the same old, same old. Though things were getting a little staid, Friday & Saturday nights at Strutz, Strathclyde Uni and Hurricanes were still an essential part of the Glasgow Psychobilly lifestyle and we were surprised they missed it. The following week they were brimming excitedly with tales of their first scooter run, "up all night", "scooter dances" etc, etc. We were initially unimpressed as we knew little about scooters, other than what we had seen in Quadrophenia, and were less than enthusiastic about all-nighters in draughty dancehalls where Psychobilly discs were only occasionally spun but, after some relentless badgering, we gave in.

One weekend, when little was happening on the Glasgow scene, Tripney, Bert, the Black Puma and I jumped in a car and followed the girls down to the Scarborough scooter run of 1987. We made sure that we parked well along the prom from the camp site as someone had tipped us off that many scooter puritans were increasingly furrowing their brows at the increasing number of scooter-run attendees turning up in cars and vans offering bullshit excuses such as "my scoots being repaired" or "honest, I've got a Lambretta at home". Anyway we were not too bothered, after all, you have to try before you buy (or so I tell the ladies).

We sneaked out of the car, got rapidly pissed then wandered amongst the masses of scooterists until the nights entertainment began. Enjoying the change of scenery, but still under-awed, we made our way to the evening venue - an underground car park. This was where our scootering baptism was to begin.

The first thing that hit me was the sheer scale of the event. Those mid-eighties runs must have counted the faithful by the thousand and Scarborough boasted a sea of skins, punks, mods and psychobillies. I had never seen so many alternative types in my life as the majority of psycho-gigs I had attended, even the Klub Foot, rarely tickled a capacity of four figures. There were punters everywhere, cramped into a tatty concrete bunker stinking of booze and piss with (almost) nobody looking to start a serious rumble.

The second factor that impressed me immensely was the music. From an early age I have always had a broad musical taste and at Scarborough we were inducted into the range of sounds which were cornerstones of the scooter scene - a touch of 60's Pop, Eighties Mod, Punk, Oi, Ska, Psycho, Motown & Northern Soul. No chart music, no dance, just a non-stop, boisterous, boot-stomping, foot shuffling classics. The good stuff kept spinning all-night: The Meteors, The Who, The Jam, Booker T, Sham 69, Desmond Dekker, King Kurt, Edwin Starr, (early) Billy Ocean... my head was spinning and my feet were burning.

We danced and drank all night and enjoyed the suitably rowdy, but friendly, atmosphere. I chatted to punters from all over the UK, and not only other psychobillies. There were no bullshit barriers between folks, everyone shared the buzz of scootering and even though we were car-driving tourists it was enough to convince us that the scooter scene was where we belonged. Strutz, Hurricanes, Vamps and Strathclyde Uni all seemed a touch stale now as weekend long music & booze bonanzas all over Britain offered a boot to their collective arse. Fuck Glasgow every weekend of our lives, apart from the odd jaunt to the Klub Foot or a Night of the Long Knives do, we were going to get two wheel burnin' round the grottiest seaside resorts blighty had to offer.

I left the venue as the sky started to tinge with daylight, thrilled by the prospect of future scootering action. That night I fell asleep, pissed and face down, outside the car. The rest of the rotters left me there so they would have more space inside. We sneaked off in the morning, burning with shame at our car-driving antics, but vowing to get scootering as soon as possible and never return on four wheels.

Not long after Scarborough we took the plunge and invested in a brand new scooter each. The Black Puma, Bert and Tripney all had good-earning jobs and got their's immediately - same colour (red) and consecutive number plates. I had to wrestle together some finance and got a small trade-in on an old motorbike which I used for my work. My scoot arrived a short time after.

We bought them from a bandito in Falkirk who really must have seen us coming as he flogged us four brand new, bright red Vespa ETS 125's. At the time the ETS was Piaggio's latest model in which some bright spark took the engine and performance of the classic Vespa PX and jammed it into the shell of a PK 50, a machine often regarded as little more than a pumped up moped. The speed and reliability was brilliant but they looked weedy, lacking the classic 'armchair on wheels' styling of the PX. The ETS was truly the betamax equivalent of a scooter.

As we were scooter-owning virgins, we set off regularly to put these new machines into action on the road but I think we all shared the unspoken belief, as we met more scooterists, that they just did not ook right. Either way we took to scootering in a big way and were constantly on the move looking out for dances or other scooter gatherings, such as the traditional Saturday afternoon visit to Mickey Oates' Clydeside scooter shop.

During one of our weekend uns, around the network of ountry roads that surround the north west of Glasgow, we stopped in the small village of Drymen for some refreshment. An ordinary looking geezer began talking to us when he noticed (probably with a smirk) our four identical scoots. In retrospect we must have looked like a troupe of two-wheeled circus performers. The guy's name was George and he claimed that a reasonable number of yokel scooterists from scattered villages in the vicinity regularly met in Drymen under the Glasgow Vespa Club (GVC) monicker. We secretly thought it unlikely that such a wide and sparsely populated area could provide much of a gathering of scoot enthusiasts but he seemed a friendly guy and he suggested that we drop in on one of their Sunday night meetings at a village boozer.

Despite our doubts, thankfully, we made a trip back to one of the club meetings and from that point on my scootering life kicked off in a big way. George introduced us to the GVC membership which at that time consisted of Jack, Louise, Shane, Richie, Gordon (future kingpin of The Amphetameanies), Robin and Stripey, a bunch of hayseeds who were all solid, well-established scooterists. Neither of them were in any way recognisable as skins, mods or psychobillies but of that other dimension of punter - the straight-up scooterist. Northern Soul loving, short-haired, scooter geezers (and geezette). We got on well almost immediately and, unlike the few scooterists we had come across in Glasgow, the had no sniffy preconceptions about psychobillies and welcomed us on board. We were voted in at the next meeting and the GVC membership was boosted by almost forty percent.

The club had a bit of history stretching back to the Sixties and had been maintained almost consistently by a middle-aged geezer named Fat Stevie, based in Balloch near Loch Lomond. Having weathered the lean years of the early to mid seventies, the club was undergoing a bit of a renaissance kickstarted by George and the rest of the hillbillies. With us on board it continued to grow as we brought Tracy, Lorna and Quentin on board then Raymie, his brother Graham and a Bearsden psycho called Ian Whiit also joined the ranks. With new enthusiastic support looking for regular scooter antics, the club was evolving rapidly and Stevie soon took a step back from the new breed.

We began to socialise almost constantly with the original GVC punters dragging along our closest psycho amigos such as Pat, Moorsy and the rest of the bams. With some of the Glasgow Psychobilly action cooling off it opened up a whole new scene. We encouraged the GVC to join us in our regular Glasgow haunts and in return they introduced us to a variety of scooter do's, Northern Soul nights and wild parties out in the sticks.

As our first year of scootering began near the end of the run season, the club activities were mostly social throughout the autumn and winter. This took the form of attending other club's dances, the odd motocross event and plenty of zipping around Glasgow waving at other scooterists. The GVC posse appeared to be well known in the scoot scene and they introduced us to other clubs such as The Coyotes, The Black Panthers, Glasgow Spectrum and The Globetrotters. As we met more scooterists we soon came to the conclusion that our ETS Vespas had to go. They got us started in the scootering lifestyle but gradually we traded in our poor investments for more traditional PX models that felt far more like the real thing.

When spring arrived, it was time to hit he national runs again - this time on scooters. Now we were on two wheels there was no desire to wimp out and go by car. At this point if you are waiting for a succession of dates, venues and travelling distances... forget it, but each run was much the same, fun, booze, spliffs, speed, getting pissed on by rain, damp tents and wearing two pair of trousers and multiple jackets for days. My run uniform was always the same: pants, jeans, army trousers and boots with a t-shirt, jumper, biker's jacket/pilot jacket combo with perhaps one spare top and clean kecks (for emergency's only). Travel light and smell like shite by the end of the run.

The old GVC punters were far more sensible with thermals, multi-layered clobber and north sea fishermen strength waterproofs. I eventually relented to some of their protective sartorial suggestions after spending days damp and experiencing toe-curling motorway moments when the rain actually seeped onto my bare bollocks. At one small club run on the Scottish island of Millport, Richie and I broke into a caravan site washroom and attempted to jam all our gear into the tumble-dryer, boots and all. That was real scootering glamour, both sitting in our damp scants in a cold outhouse with a hangover.

Millport was also memorable as I ended up in Clydebank hospital after falling off my scooter while mimicking the arse-grab of another GVC punter while heading down the dual-carriageway. Though lost in a boozy haze of two-stroke and Buckfast, other runs which jog the memory were our first return to Scarborough on two wheels (I got ill from licking Buckfast off the promenade), Girvan (always good jock fun and easy to get to), Rhyl (a fucking disaster), Morecombe (a fucking success) and Skegness (pissed and pissing on the top of an open-topped tour bus with Raymie and Richie).

Shamefacedly, I must admit that I often gave a miss to runs that were well south of the border such as the Isle of Wight, Gt. Yarmouth and Brighton but I just found it too monotonous creeping down the motorway through the night at a steady 55 mph. Hardcore scooterists may recoil in horror at this disclosure but be honest, its fucking boring. Scooters are at their best for urban cruising not long-haul journeys and anyway, the barren stretch of road between Glasgow and Carlisle would drive anyone nuts - especially going up and down it every three weeks.

The scootering experience during the runs season was intense and most of the time you were either preparing for a run or recovering from one. At that time I remained in a part-time job purely because I needed almost every third Friday off for scootering activities (and almost equal Mondays off to recover). When the run season ended we launched into a series of GVC meetings, parties and club events just to keep the buzz going. I even began to slip slowly into the role of scooter boy with my quiff gradually decreasing to a short flat-top then skinhead. Psychobilly became only a part of my lifestyle and musical interest and though psycho sounds and bands were a key part of the Eighties scooter scene, I was consumed by scootering and decide to take it to the next level and customise my scooter.

One weekend I stripped my Vespa down to its frame with the intention of painting it, adding murals & lettering then chopping it. I had the theme all planned, a chrome plated, bright purple tribute to my early trash heroes The Vibes and The Purple Things (geddit?). Then something bizarre happened that I still can not explain. Like Samson's barnet my dismantled scoot mysteriously drained away my enthusiasm for the scootering game. As my progress was so slow, and I was unable to get back on the road I began to miss the odd run or club meeting. Within weeks I had accepted a new job up north and I left Glasgow, and my PX (in pieces), behind. I never rode again in the nineties and my GVC days were over.

Chapter 9:
'Just when I thought I was out... they pull me back in'

Some years after leaving school I got my first real job after pissing about on youth training schemes and signing on. It was working in the newly opened branch of a major record retail chain in my home town Cumbernauld. As I have always embraced a wide range of music, it never seemed like real work and I rapidly progressed to a store manager's position within the first year.

Being young and dopey, I had no set career path (I still don't) and before I knew it I had accepted a manager's job in the bollock-freezing town of Inverness, Scotland's most northern outpost of above ghost-town size. As this was my first position of note I assumed the theme was to dig in and work like a madman for the bosses. I worked non-stop, from early morn to late at night, seven days a week almost constantly. During this time socialising was out of the question and tending my quiff became secondary. My hair grew into a nondescript side-shed and my wardrobe lost almost all its Psychobilly sartorial splendour. I had become Joe Soap but was too busy to notice.

After three months of this graft, and finding no signs of Psychobilly or scootering life in Inverness, I took a rare opportunity to go back home for a few days. Around this time Bob was recently wed and keeping a low profile, Tripney was in London working on Canary Wharf and Big Bert was beginning to drift into the rave scene. Raymie got in touch and we headed into Glasgow for a big night out in the traditional style - a carry out at his house, a spin of some psycho discs then onto the bus with a bottle of Buckfast each.

As 'Hurricanes', Glasgow's premier Psychobilly watering hole was no more, an attempt had been made to find a new gathering place. A boozer called McSorley's was the venue and here an uneasy truce was in effect between the regulars and the city's be-quiffed faithful, who drank upstairs in a small attic-type area. When we arrived I recognised a few faces and said my hellos. I also noticed the occasionally punter we had experienced 'poor relations' with before but as the scene was shrinking it now appeared to be a new era of 'billy brotherhood. There were also a good few new faces (to me) who Raymie introduced me too. Among them were a bunch of hillbillies from Kilmarnock who were then becoming Scotland's most famous Psychobilly export, The Termites.

We settled down to some serious drinking and I soon realised that my old amigos and these newer additions to the clan were all good mates and obviously used to regular sessions together. Their adventures in Psychobilly had continued while I was busting my ass, like a mug, in some bland record store (that did not even stock any Psychobilly or Trash). I felt like an observer of the proceedings, a tourist, a visitor to the realm of psycho - I had let the faith slip.

As I sat there, I was sure one of the guys who I had just met shot me a quick glance. 'Who's this square?', it seemed to say. With my flat barnet and 'Top Man' gear, I suddenly felt like an outsider in a scene which I had been part of since the early days. At this point it hit me straight between the eyes, "Fuck This!", my rockin' days were far from over in my early twenties. I had to get back into it.

The next day I travelled back to Inverness, listening to The Meteors, King Kurt, Torment, Demented and Skitzo all the way. I handed my bosses some bullshit excuse about having to get back to Glasgow asap, and got my haircut. To finally exorcise the squareifying grip that ole northern town had placed on me, I cut the sleeves of my denim jacket and plonked the rest in a bucket of bleach. The record store bosses got their revenge by sending me to their tiniest bum-crack of a store in Irvine (no offence, but...) but I was back in the big smoke, quiffed up once again and as an added bonus Hurricane's was about to be reborn as Glasgow's newest Psychobilly home from home - Richard's.

Despite being sent to work in the back of beyond I was glad to get back to the Glasgow psycho life. I genuinely felt part of it again and things were almost the same as they had been, the scene was a little smaller but we now hung together en-masse and many of the old divisions were forgotten.

Strathclyde Uni had been refitted and became decidedly unfriendly to the Psychobilly posse but fuck them and their polished ponce parlour, we moved to the suitably tatty Glasgow Tech Students Union. Stick that up yer bar receipts. More importantly, Hurricanes had reopened with a new name, Richard's, and a new owner (a guy called Richard - surprisingly!). After a few weeks of noticing nosey psychobillies peeking into his, relatively quiet, new boozer to check it out he approached us and after hearing our tales of Hurricanes' past as Glasgow's premier 'billy boozer he welcomed us back. Quickly, this basement booze-hole reached new heights playing a mix of good tunes and Psychobilly favourites while introducing live music & karaoke and attracting large numbers of pissed-up office girls.

This was the scene as the Eighties drew to a close and around this time I felt that Psychobilly, in general, was experiencing its second wave. The glory days of The Meteors and King Kurt on major record labels were gone. The Klub Foot was no more and many psychos had drifted into scootering or football thuggery, while the fad-chasers had simply jumped aboard the next bandwagon. A number of original psycho & Trash bands had changed personnel, changed direction or simply given up - R.I.P The Styng-Rites, The Sting-Rays, and Tall Boys.

Despite this, it was not a time of a scene slowly dying. In fact the whole network of bands, fans and gigs was becoming leaner but stronger. Those passing through on the way to normality had passed the fuck through, leaving only the faithful still standing. Still treading the boards were the likes of The Frantic Flintstones, Torment, The Coffin Nails and of course The Meteors. A whole host of new bands had also sprung up on the dusty trails between London's 'Sir George Robey', Stoke's 'Billy's' and 'The Charlotte' in Leicester. Bands like The Klingonz were bringing an even bigger punk influence into Psychobilly and a host of euro-bands, such as Mad Sin and The Nekromantix, were giving a whole new international flavour to the scene. Even the US was sending over classic rockin' in the shape of The Quakes, Elvis Hitler and The Hellbillys.

The Meteors were still in command of the Psychobilly crown and in a strange twist of fate my amigo Raymie answered an ad in Melody Maker in which Mr Fenech announced auditions for a new drummer. Being a complete Meteors fanatic and ace psycho-drummer he was nudged into making the trip south for a drumskin rattling test of skill. He returned home only to pack his bags as P. Paul liked his style and before we could really register our amazement at Raymie's monumental achievement he was off on tour in Japan.

Psychobilly festivals galore in the early nineties. L-R: Emmet(?), Pat the Hat, Twinger & Bruno at Hemsby? Night of the Long Knives? Who Knows?

In between spreading the Psychobilly gospel across the globe, The Meteors rarely played many of the multi-band psycho shows across Blighty as they (and the Kattle) appeared to have little time for many other bands. Always ready to fill in a headline gap, were fellow Psychobilly pioneers Demented Are Go. I have always been a big fan of these Welsh mental out-patients, since I first came across them on the 'Hell's Bent On Rockin' album, and they had always been a popular act, as far back as the Klub Foot days, outrunning almost all of their early label partners (whatever happened to Rochee & the Sarnos?). Soon they were gaining a worldwide reputation second only to the mighty Meteors, especially as The Guana Batz were beginning to slip slightly off the radar. Most gigs I attended featured a sea of Demented t-shirts and painted biker's jackets and the band were often headliners, always putting on a good show and lifting heavily from their back catalogue of true psycho classics.

Arguably, the brightest stars of this Psychobilly 'second wave' has to be The Klingonz, The Klingz, The Kling Klong Klan. I was first introduced to the band by my old Kilsyth buddy, Tripney, who had met them out on the London psycho scene. He also did a bit of driving for them and it was his cow-coloured van which appeared on the cover of their 'Flange' album. By the time we met them Strangy, their original bass player, had left and Eddie (later of Demented & Thee Exit Wounds) was on board.

I have no recollection of when I first heard The Klingonz or whether it was on vinyl or live but from the start I thought their albums were genuine originals and they 'always' put on a wild show (no half-measures). In fact I have never seen a band focus so much on getting psyched-up for gigs. Offstage they may have been happy to fuck about but in the run up to performing live they appeared deadly serious about giving the punters an excellent show, everytime. And with the amount of live work they battered through they could always turn it on and leave the punters in no doubt that they had been 'Klinged' by the end of the night.

Specialist record labels, such as Nervous, Fury, Raucous, Dojo & ID, were also keeping the scene booming by continuing to release a fine selection of debut albums, signing up new Euro-talent and continuing to deliver a steady flow of compilations featuring psychos old and new. Although any major label interest was dead, Psychobilly was in rude health and new bands had an even greater chance of being tied down to vinyl (at last!). Soon the likes of The Lost Souls, The Hangmen, The Surfin' Wombatz and The Highliners were elbowing their way into the record collections of British psychos.

In particular, compilation

albums such as 'Psycho Tendencies' and the 'Zorch' series spread the net a little further to include regulars on the psycho scene along with a few bands who shone briefly then disappeared into the dark annals of psycho history like The Shakin' Bones, The Sugar Puff Demons and Grovelhog. And lets not forget the fanzine titles, such as the sadly missed 'Deathrow Database', which kept the scene alive during its second wave and into the leaner times ahead. At the turn of the decade the UK scene may have been a little smaller than the mid/late Eighties boom but, with the rest of the world getting on board, there were further good times ahead for the psycho nation.

Chapter 11:
When The Caravan's a Rockin'....(The Hemsby Experience).

If further proof were needed that Psychobilly was in rude health, one fine morning a big, brown envelope dropped through my mail-hole. It heralded the first ever Psychobilly weekender in Hemsby, near Gt. Yarmouth. At the time this was a new concept to me although I soon learned that Rockabilly and Rock 'n' Roll weekenders have been regular events for decades. So how about all this: three days, three nights, a pile of psycho bands, crates of booze, stacks of doobies, all crammed into some manky, out of season, post-war holiday chalets. Hi-de-fucking-hi, let's go!

After doing the rounds in the pub with the booking form most of the geezers jumped at the chance. This was to be an unmissable splodge on the Psychobilly landscape. One Friday morning, just after opening time, in April 1990 we all gathered in Richard's Bar and began supping. Soon after, Stix pulled up in his camouflage-painted mini-bus. We threw in some diesel money and crammed into it. There was little luggage other than a bag each of T-shirts & jeans, some crates of lager and bottles of Buckfast in case 'them English' did not sell the Scottish bam's favourite tipple. The organisers suggested we bring some other 'essentials' such as sleeping bags and bog roll. The toilet paper was a definite but all those little white bags of powder circulating among the group suggested many of the kipping sacks would remain unopened.

Heading into the unknown, I was joined by Raymie (my old-timey Cumbernauld amigo), Pat (first of the Glasgow posse to extend the hand of friendship, way back), Moorsy (false teeth, tattoos and party starter), Kev the Gerbil (I've no idea what it means?), Scotty (up all night, and all day etc), Easterhouse Ian (from Easterhouse), Tonto (Glasgow's Rockabilly legend), Brian (very early leather trouser wearer) and Stix. We had all travelled to gigs down south many times before but a long-weekend, in our own P.O.W. camp chalets, seemed a totally unique concept. Sure the digs would turn out to be as spartan as possible but Hemsby number one would leave us desperate for more.

As we sped down the motorway the party started - joints

were sparked and the screw-tops of Buckfast bottles were vigorously twisted off. Easterhouse Ian had perfected a sheepdog whistle which always sent field loads of sheep dashing into the distance and pelleting themselves as we passed. We pissed ourselves consistently at this until well over the border (it must have been good weed). Cutting through the Midlands we were getting more gassed as darkness fell but, sober as a judge, Stix kept the foot to the floor and hurtled us towards Psychobilly Valhalla.

After a few pit stops at motorway services (or robbin' bastard points as they are known) the spirits began to sag a little in the wee small hours and most of the punters in the back lapsed into unconsciousness. Stix and I chatted quietly upfront as he continued to tear up the road while a Psychobilly soundtrack I had prepared parped constantly from the speakers.

As dawn broke and the van trundled on it was psycho-breakfasts all round - two packets of crisps, a Mars bar, a doobie and a freshly opened can of lager. A wash, and fresh socks & pants, were far from everyone's minds - hairy teeth and dirty dicks were in (scooter run style). The early morn saw us approach Gt. Yarmouth, then fanny about looking for Hemsby itself. Was it a town? Was it on the beach? Eventually after haranguing a few locals we found it. Achtung! Donner und blitzen! We were at Colditz-on-sea.

First up we were met by grinning Del from Fury Records. This was my first meeting with the label supremo but (as I would find out in later dealings) he was always the same - a number one geezer, open and friendly.

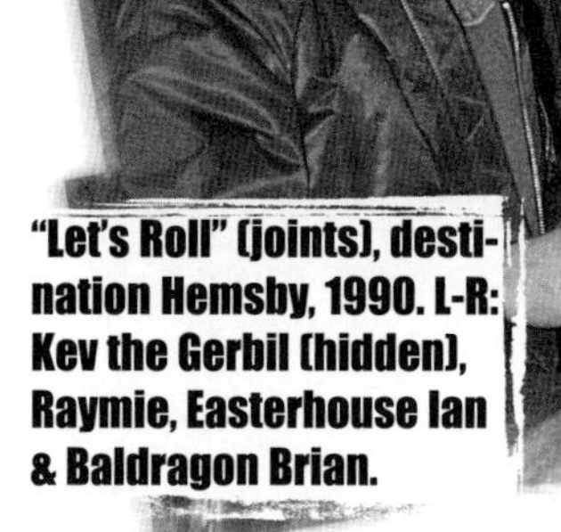

"Let's Roll" (joints), destination Hemsby, 1990. L-R: Kev the Gerbil (hidden), Raymie, Easterhouse Ian & Baldragon Brian.

As we were one of the earliest groups to arrive he made us welcome, booked us in, pointed to our chalets and told us, as he told everyone, not to wreck the place or our deposit would be kaput. We checked out the final band line-up, scratched on an old notice board in reception and the buzz began to build. The weekend started here!

Because of our early arrival, the place was still eerily quiet with only a few other psychos shuffling around. We had been allotted three downstairs chalets pretty close to each other. The chalets themselves were long concrete blocks, two storeys high. Each block contained around fourteen chalets and were positioned, with three other blocks, onto a basic grass square. This set up of blocks appeared all over the site. Fuck spending the summer here with ma, pa & granny but the holiday season was over and, as the chalets filled, a ready-made psycho community was being formed for a three-day shebang.

We did not even bother to argue over beds as sleeping was not really on the agenda. We threw our bags in the bedroom and began filling the fridge with our carry out. I was in with Raymie, Stix and Tonto. Across the grass square was Scotty, Brian and The Gerbil next door to Pat, Moorsy and Ian. Tripney was missing but

Caister Caravan Wreckers AGM. Pissed & proud. L-R: Tripney, Bracko, Scotty & The Black Puma.

 61

he was making his way up from London on the specially chartered psycho-coach service. As the clock hit noon we were well on the way to being pissed.

For that reason, the majority of the weekend slipped by in a blur but I still remember the awe I felt at being part of a gathering of possibly a thousand other psychos (1000 Kats!) from all over the world, boozing, wrecking, toking, shagging and simply just hanging around together in the grounds of this, relatively small, holiday camp. The atmosphere was electric with great bands playing mere yards from our digs and sussed bouncers who could distinguish between rowdy behaviour and serious violence. There was total freedom to float between the venue and a score of in-chalet parties and, as we were in an enclosed private camp, we could booze it up outside, inside and even arse-down in five inches of stagnant water in the kiddie's paddling pool.

I never went outside the holiday centre once during the whole event as everything I wanted was contained within the (barbed wire) perimeter fence. I enjoyed the whole weekend so much I was almost scared to sleep in case I missed any action (or had my eyebrows shaved off... or worse). By the time Monday came we were all totally fucked and made a half-arsed attempt to tidy the wrecked chalets in a vague hope of securing the return of our deposit. As we trundled back up the road, a little quieter, we were already planning our return as we knew this would become an essential part of the Psychobilly lifestyle. Rumbles 2 & 3 soon came and went in a similar excellent blur of good times and great music but the 4th Big Rumble was shaping up to be a little more special.

The 1st Big Rumble - on the road, 1990. L-R: Raymie, Scotty & Bracko.

62

Ironically as the decade was ending and Psychobilly was flourishing in its second wave I was again starting to lose the plot a bit in my continuing bid for rock stardom, taking my short, sharp shock methods to the extreme with my then current combo Hell, Death & Breakfast. Unfortunately the name was as good as it got as we knocked out growling speed metal in a Napalm Death stylee, unaware that early psycho legends Skitzo were also moving in that direction. The band featured Kev, Stix and I (in long wigs) along with two local metallers James Blast and Heatnin' Plumbin'. Apart from a rather entertaining live video we made in concert (when one local half-wit broke his leg), how is this for a speed metal overview of our career - shite!

With Hell, Death & Breakfast soon in the bin, I felt we should carry on where The Razorbacks left off but this time go for a more authentic Psychobilly sound. I was sure this was a time when we could get noticed as record labels such as Nervous, Fury, Link and Raucous were throwing the net out a bit further and signing bands from all over the UK, Ireland and Europe. Fellow jockabillies The Termites were on a roll and with a plentiful supply of compilation albums flooding the market as well, I was keen that we did not miss the boat this time. Kev and Stix agreed so we began our hunt for a bass player.

The hunt started and ended at Richard's one Friday night. We were talking about the abrupt end of Hell, Death & Breakfast some weeks before, when we had performed an abysmal set supporting Glasgow's Macc Lads - The Bad Men, then disbanded backstage. Our public shaming was the source of much merriment amongst our Psychobilly mates who confirmed that they thought we had been utter shite all along. I mentioned that we were forming a new psycho band and in need of a bass player when Murray immediately offered his services. He was a quality four-string plank-spanker who had played in Glasgow psycho band, The Talismen (along with Raymie and Pat the Hat), a few years earlier but now his bass was gathering dust. We welcomed him onboard then got him along to our first practice session.

Murray fitted in well immediately, he had a solid 'walking the dog' electric bass style with a strong Meteors influence and could handle anything we threw at him. More importantly, he was a good mate from the early Glasgow 'billy days and always maintained an immaculate quiff. As we were all relatively relaxed together, and had a reasonably shared idea of the sound we wanted, the tunes soon started to flow. I penned a few songs using regular Psychobilly themes such as teenage lust, mad pigs and American cars. Stix, a fellow devotee of the Macc Lads, wrote some remarkably detailed filthy lyrics while Murray provided a substantial back catalogue of death, murder and graveyard themes. Kev, never a true believer in Psychobilly's lyrical genius, kept his pen to himself but supplied a continuous barrage of twangs, riffs and guitar solos.

More importantly, we needed a name that would illustrate our psycho-hillbilly sound. At the time I was listening to a lot of rockin' country music especially Charlie Daniels, he of 'The Devil Went Down To Georgia' fame. The standout track on his, then current, 'Simple Man' album was a Reagan-esque romp called 'What This World Needs is a Few More Rednecks'. It was a rockin' track which tackled the fact that, in the States, 'Redneck' was a dirty word with racist connotations but (he claimed) Rednecks were really just America's common working punters.

At the time we never contemplated the deeper meaning of the name, The Rednecks sounded good for our sound and it (at the time) meant fuck all over in the UK. 'What This World Needs...' was knocked up a gear and became one of our many cover

Pre-performance warm-up at the 4th Big Rumble, Gt. Yarmouth, 1991.

versions. With a name and thirty minutes of racket, prepared and rehearsed, The Rednecks were ready to play their small part in jockin', rockin' history.

Our first gig was in September 1990 at Glasgow's Rooftops Nightclub, a sometime rockin' venue which in the olden days hosted the cream of Psychobilly talent and offered us jocks early glimpses of the live brilliance of The Meteors, King Kurt, The Guana Batz and Frenzy. Raymie, Pat and I were dabbling in live band booking under the monicker of Deathshead Promotions and keeping the nepotism quota high, The Rednecks were to foot the bill of our first production, a Long Tall Texans gig with The Termites in support. That first performance was well received but a bit of a blur for me as I jumped between collecting tickets at the door, performing and attempting to DJ through the night.

After our rushed attempt to prepare for The Texans gig, The Rednecks moved back into a more leisurely mode which was to be an early sign of rot. Quite simply it always took us fucking ages to get things together at any time, especially crucial elements such as new songs, promoting demos and generally chasing gigs. This had been

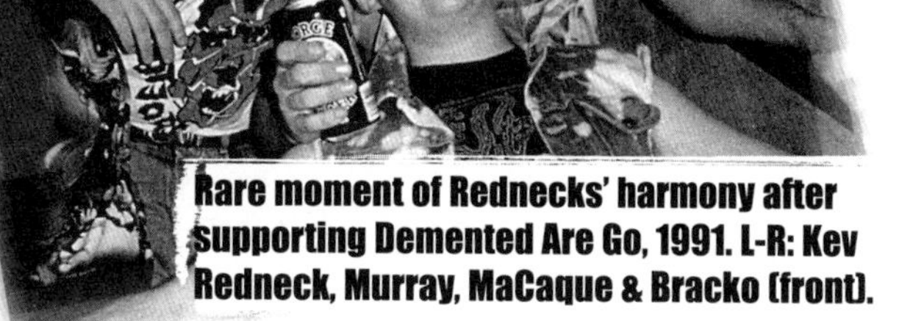

Rare moment of Rednecks' harmony after supporting Demented Are Go, 1991. L-R: Kev Redneck, Murray, MaCaque & Bracko (front).

a factor back in The Razorback days and unwittingly we slipped back into it with The Rednecks who, throughout our short career, would only really play gigs when promoters approached us. We were inactive, not proactive. Not (only) because we were lazy swines but we all had other things going on such as Stix career and romancing, Murray's impending fatherhood, my interests in film, TV & music and I still do not know what Kev gets up to on cold, winter nights (but it sure keeps him busy).

As if to illustrate our slacker attitude to gigging, our next gig was seven months later, again a Deathshead promotion, this time supporting the mighty Demented Are Go. This gig was far more memorable as I got some punters to cover my promoter duties and then kicked backstage with the Welsh wonders drinking our shared rider, 48 cans of out-of-date 'Charger' lager (foul bilge-water, about 1.5% proof). Just to keep things interesting, Demented's lead singer Mark disappeared and had to be hunted down, amongst Glasgow's meths-swilling hobos, before the soundcheck.

This was our first real introduction to Glasgow's Psychobilly faithful and our intro song 'Razorback Attack' got things off to a flying start, closely followed by a high-speed cover of The Purple Things' 'Wild Man' (Pedants note: I know this is an old 60's psych original but our version was based on The Purple Things rendition. Post-modern or what!). I was really enjoying this gig, having a bit of stage to move about on for a change, and I felt our sound was tighter than any previous band I had fronted, mainly due to Kev, Murray and Stix musical ability as opposed to my often rambled warblings. I always place performance over musical anal retention

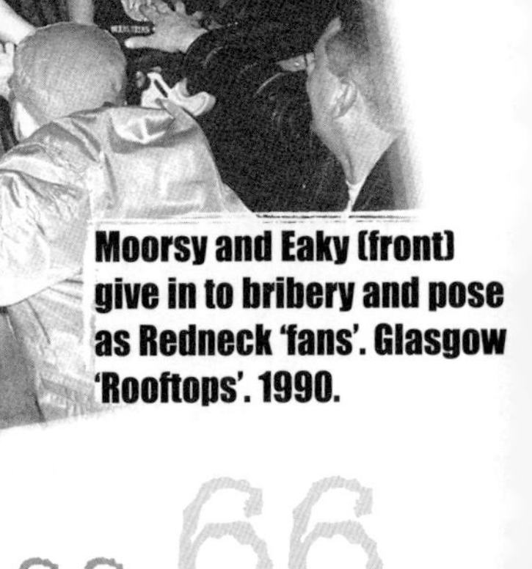

Moorsy and Eaky (front) give in to bribery and pose as Redneck 'fans'. Glasgow 'Rooftops'. 1990.

and would often skip verses or sing over solos if I got carried away while thrusting my bollocks at the audience but the rest of the band always covered my gaffes seamlessly.

I also believe in hitting the punters with some good lively sounds as soon as the band hits the stage and jolting them out of their complacency for the support band (which we often were). Fuck those slow-building beginnings, keep the set moving racily throughout and end on a speedy, vibrant note. For these reasons, Redneck's stage appearances - like all my old bands - were brief encounters but any new band littering a stage for any more than thirty minutes is wasting their, and the audiences, time. Hit them hard and fast then get the fuck offstage. Using this method, if you are good the punters do not know what hit them and if you are shite they do not get time to dwell on it. That night we did exactly that, had a thoroughly enjoyable gig, but got off sharpish and made way for Demented, the real reason folks had coughed up cash that night.

In an unaccustomed flurry of activity we took to the stage again, mere weeks after the Demented support, to headline a Halloween bash at our local boozer Richard's. Being as it was on the night of witchery, fancy dress was in order and we took to the stage in Clockwork Orange gear and played to a selection of circus freaks, naughty nurses, vicars, cavemen, ballet dancers and Chuck Berry lookalikes. Our performance was slightly off, mainly due to me missing huge chunks of lyrics, but I was bamboozled by this tiny pub stacked to bursting point with heavily disguised psychobillies and psychobetties. I was trying to work out who everybody was and my mind was wandering but Kev, Murray and Stix disguised my fuck-ups by keeping the set tighter than a highlander's wallet (again!).

I felt that night was a point in time when the Glasgow scene was at its tightest. Sure the numbers were down from the mid-Eighties glory days but almost everyone knew each other and nobody felt uncomfortable about fannying around, in fancy dress, in front of anyone else. From then on the distilled spirit of Glasgow's psycho-scene would gradually be watered down and, even at future gigs, I never saw so many of those folks together again in one place.

After another five month period of inactivity we kicked ourselves in the arse, recorded a six track demo and set about promoting it to the UK's Psychobilly bigwigs. The results were almost immediate and off the back of our promotion blitz we secured a one-off EP deal with Del at Fury Records and lined up a series of gigs at Billy's in Stoke, The Fourth Big Rumble Weekender at GT. Yarmouth and The Sir George Robey in ole London town.

While half pissed at an early Hemsby weekender I had approached Del from Fury, told him of The Rednecks and promised to send him a demo. After recovering back home, I got together a tape and some publicity bumf and posted it to the big man as promised. Pretty soon after, he phoned back, told me of his plans to release a series of limited edition, coloured-vinyl E.P's and offered us a one-off single deal. At first I panicked, assuming we would have to foot the bill to travel down to London and re-record the tracks. We had been such skinflints in the studio that after our recording session we chose not to pay for the original master tapes and our only source for the demos was a single, high-quality, audio cassette. Del assured me that they could master the single from that tape and I posted it down.

At this point, many musos, band members and studio engineers may howl in disbelief at this (relatively) poor source for a vinyl release. However, I have always had the punk idealism that bashing out some songs on the cheap is better than wasting cash (which we did not have anyway) creating an immaculate sonic symphony that sounds over-produced and boring. Del was not about to cough up recording fees anyway, so my feeling was that if he is happy with it and wants to release it who are we to

The Rednecks 'For A Few Rednecks More' EP: Fury Records (FEP 702), 1991.

stamp our feet like petulant brats and demand studio time. Though Kev and Stix felt strongly that the demo did not do full justice to their twanging and banging abilities, I managed to persuade them that in true Punk spirit 'owt' was better than 'nowt' and the EP's production went ahead.

The tracks we chose were the cream (or best we had) of The Redneck's repertoire. First off was an old leftover from our early days as The Razorbacks, the suitably monikered 'Razorback Attack'. This tune, to us, was as old as father time's beard but still a lively track which was most suited to a bout of bedroom wreckin'. I had penned the lyrics which were mostly nonsense with a vague 'Mad Max' influence and it was our earliest original tune with a straight-up Psychobilly beat.

Track two was 'Jailbait', still a big favourite of mine, which I felt was a fine blend of Psychobilly and Garage Punk. If we had continued to knock out tracks in this vein I am sure that our future sound would have been different. Its heavy, almost surf sound, successfully drew attention away from some of the more 'Carry On' style lyrics which I had penned concerning teen lust. Still, this track would be resurrected (more of that later).

Flip over to Side Two to be greeted by 'Line Up Linda', our most blatant Macc Lads tribute which, for better or for worse, sent The Rednecks on a course that was to remain laden with smut, toilet humour and a ragbag of Punk and Psychobilly influences. I am sure you can guess at the lyrical content and 'No' it was not written about anyone we knew (honest!).

Bringing the whole affair to an end was our most bizarre track, 'Hand Job Baby'. Although I have a great love for this track and its wickedly filthy lyrics (penned by Stix), I believe this song had the power to alienate the majority of any psycho audience. Apart from the few bursts of speed which it contains, in reality it had always been a slow (almost funk) workout of progressive rock proportions. In rehearsals we regularly lost it and indulged ourselves in twenty minute renditions of the song, endless jams with constant changes of pace and solos on all instruments (there was even a reggae version). Playing the tune live, in its entirety, would have been suicide but even the drastically shortened version on the single must still have left many listeners asking the poignant question, 'What the fuck was that?'. Anyway, any song which rhymes 'like' with 'pork spike' has to have some merit.

Having posted the master tape the matter of publishing was next on the agenda. Del directed us to Roy Williams, keeper of the Nervous Records empire. The majority of Fury's roster seemed to go through Nervous' Publishing division so we were happy to follow suit. We got the paperwork through and, in a fit of brotherly solidarity, we decided not to break the lyrics and music credits up into their constituent parts. All tracks were credited to Brackenridge / McAllister / Murray / Younger, so we were all due an equal share of the royalties which were to roll in (tee! hee!). Although Stix and I had created the lyrics, we often built songs around existing bass and guitar riffs so I always believed the process to be an equal collaboration anyway. Besides, what would most folks remember about a song such as 'Razorback Attack', the rockin' tune or the dopey lyrics? You tell me.

With the record and its label info in order, the final stage of production was the creation of a full-colour picture cover. Del was happy for us to produce our own cover as long as it carried the requisite Fury info, and Kev was already experienced in graphic design, so we got to work. My initial idea was to feature the four of us on the front cover, pictured in the waiting room of a VD clinic, and to title the EP 'Line Up Linda & other stories' but Del and Roy nearly wet the bed when they received our proposal and claimed this idea would render the disc difficult to distribute. Maybe I am being naive but I thought this cover design was pretty mild by Psychobilly standards but regardless of this we relented and we left the job in Kev's capable hands.

We had yet to encounter our first serious photo session so now seemed like the right time. Alyn, a mate of ours, was a dab hand at snapping so we organised a photo session at an old farm in Kilsyth. Big Bert knew the farmer and he gave us 'free range' of the grounds and farm buildings. When we arrived we realised that some sort of structure, and a few prepared ideas, are essential for any publicity shoot as we wasted the first roll of film standing around awkwardly while Alyn tried to get us to relax. If we had thought of a theme, or look, that we wanted maybe we could have got down to it a little quicker. Thank fuck he was not charging hundreds by the hour like the top snappers and had been tempted by the promise of a few beers and cash for his expenses. The main problem was

WITH

THE KLINGONZ

!!!!SPECIAL GUESTS!!!!

THE cottonfield boys

★ AS ADVERTISED ON T.V ★

THE REDNECKS

DEATHSHE(A)D. Promoting Psychobilly North of the border 1991.

+ PSYCHOBILLY AND ROCKABILLY SOUNDS

SUNDAY 30TH SEPT.

ROOFTOPS, GLASGOW

TICKETS £5

LATE LICENCE

DOORS OPEN 7:30pm

that we knew what we did not want but we did not know what we did want (if that makes any sense at all).

Generally, Psychobilly photos up to that period had mostly fell into three categories: the whole band staring moodily at the camera, the band playing (or appearing to play) live or the band dicking around. These snaps, apart from the ones in concert, are usually either in a graveyard (Skitzo and The Coffin Nails were early pioneers), in a back alley or beside a yankee car (usually someone else's). The other standard was the band captured, in any combination of the above, posing with their instruments.

The moody staring pose was not really for us. We tried a few variations on this theme but, in my opinion, the front cover of The Meteors 'Wrecking Crew' album was the benchmark for a genuinely menacing look so we would be fools to ape it (besides, only Murray had a donkey jacket). Live photos were also out as most of our mates were always too pissed at our gigs to take quality snaps and we did not really want to highlight the lack of jostling wreckers in front of the stage.

Although I would have loved to have played the 'wacky' card, no jiggery-pokery flowed on the day and no ale was supped to loosen the atmosphere as I develop a squint after only a few pints. Yet again, I felt the standard for whacko poses had already been set at an impossibly high standard with The Termites star-turn appearance on the back cover of the 'Psycho Tendencies' album as four winos dossing in the street (a classic band portrait). With graveyards, Cadillacs and standing with our instruments miles from a power source also poo-pooed, we plodded on with a selection of poses amongst cow sheds, hay bales and milking machines. The final result was a set of po-faced poses which still make me titter today but we managed to salvage a few suitable ones which were passed over to Kev to work his magic.

Weeks later a pile of copies of The Rednecks' single, 'For A Few Rednecks More' popped through my door and I perused this seven-inch excitedly. It was well produced and pressed in garish red-vinyl and it was a real buzz to have finally made it on to record without resorting to pressing it ourselves. This crisp pile of EPs did not last for long as, after distributing equal copies to the other 'Necks, many of our mates also wanted a freebie copy (skinflint bastards) and instead of using them for their intended purpose of promotion, I dished them out to the tightwads. However, I kept a few and then our promotional blitz (a handful of gigs) began in earnest.

No offence to the good folks of Stoke but had Billy's club not existed, it is a town I would not have had much reason to visit. Providing some excellent stomping extravaganzas north of Watford, Billy's was basically a room above a boozer which from inside looked like an old church or school-hall with a stage which appeared to be constructed from old blackboards and beer crates. The club was run on a regular basis by SGB Entertainments and was always a good pit-stop for live Psychobilly-starved jocks. It always seemed to pull a good crowd and it gave us a closer alternative than London for multi line-up psycho action.

My first memories of Billy's are a bit vague as a team of us travelled down together in a van for a gig headlined by Demented. I was not, at the time, the owner of a valid driver's license so I was boozing all the way down the motorway and I was pissed by the time we entered the club. Despite remembering little, it was a great night and many of the regulars were friendly enough. Not friendly enough, however, to give eight pissed porridge munchers a floor to crash on, so (yet again) we spent the night in the van. As was often the case, forward planning was rarely employed and consisted of Plan A: hoping that some kind soul would offer us some floorspace to collapse on, or Plan B: the infinitely superior hope that you would get a bunk-up and a warm bed. Neither happened very often (at least that is what I am telling you, dirty pervs!).

My next trip to Stoke's mecca of stomping is slightly easier to recollect as The Rednecks were playing as part of a series of gigs 'promoting' the new single. Stix, Kev and I travelled down to the gig, along with the Black Puma, in yet another of Stix diesel-powered love machines. Murray opted for the slightly more civilised option of car travel with his wife and another couple. We were bottom of the bill to Demented, The Coffin Nails and The Hangmen. Despite our early billing, it went well and the crowd were excellent. As soon as I got offstage I drunk myself into oblivion and yet another night was spent face down in the back of Stix' van with only a pile of unsold Rednecks' singles as a pillow.

The high point of this promotional blitz followed soon after a Stoke reappearance when Del asked as down to appear at the 4th

Bottom of the bill...again! Playing with some of Psychobillie's finest, 1991.

Frantic Flintstones

Yabba dabba doo guys

MAD SIN

- Psycho maniacs from Berlin, Germany.

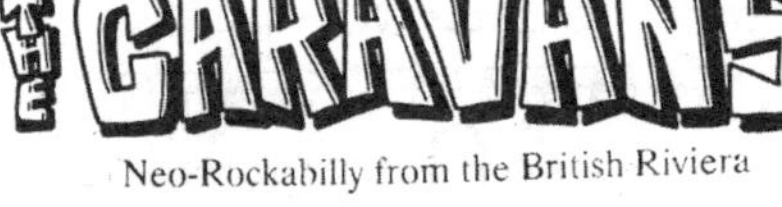

Neo-Rockabilly from the British Riviera

NEKROMANTIX

Danish psycho

ELMERS SHOTGUN

Psycho band from California, U.S.A.

PSYCHO BUNNIES

Sexy psycho from Wisconsin, U.S.A.

CELLMATES

Neo-Rockabilly inmates from Leicester

- Psycho band from Walsall

Psycho band from Scotland

Radiacs

Psycho band from Sheffield

the ARRGHONAUTS

Rock'n'Horror

Shakin' vacs

HOOVERBILLY

SELF DESTRUCT

London Punk band

Big Rumble in Gt. Yarmouth. At last we had the chance to reach a European (and beyond) audience in one fell swoop. This time we were keen to put a bit of effort into our pre-gig preparations, so we actually had a few rehearsals and even crafted a few new songs into our tired set. In addition to this, I created a large placard, emblazoned with the slogan 'Line Up!', which I intended to wave at the punters in a music-hall attempt to induce them into a singalong chorus of our tune 'Line Up Linda'. I also purchased a large wooden bog brush which I could brandish during our live rendition of 'Drop The Log' - a new song dedicated to 'dropping the kids off at the pool' (Editor's Note for the hard of thinking: doing a shite).

We travelled down to the weekender in a small convoy of the band, wives, girlfriends and the Glasgow regulars (mainly consisting of the Easterhouse and Kirkintilloch contingents). We had already planned to attend the Rumble anyway, so the free accomodation we got as a band gave us a bit more cash for beer and trash. By now, the Big Rumble had moved away from the lovable concrete bunker position at Hemsby to Vauxhall Caravan Park a venue a little nearer to the town which offered the high-class gypsy lifestyle in static caravans. Although just as good as the old site, the caravan's construction of tin, plywood and plastic would prove to be far less resistant to a solid weekend of wreckin' and rockin'.

For many of us, it was business as usual as we arrived on the Friday (half-pissed) and immediately cracked open the beers and sparked up joints. We were soon informed that our live appearance was to be that night. Not an ideal position in the weekend's line-up as many of the London buses and Euro-punters often did not arrive until later in the evening. While many were unpacking their pyjamas and looking for their caravans, we were onstage playing to a small, but responsive, crowd.

Although our early slot was a bit disappointing we gave them our best, as even a reduced Big Rumble audience was far larger than the crowd at most of our other gigs. Besides, our hybrid psycho-metal-Macc Lads-punk was an acquired taste and I am sure, on first hearing, that many of the Rumblers probably questioned what they were getting dished up on this first night of psycho revelry. Regardless of this, we got a good reaction and even a few half-hearted 'Line Up, Line Up' chants when I waved my sign in the air.

The high point of the gig for me was when the entire Glasgow crew arrived at the front of the stage (half-way through the set... the lazy bastards) and took off their jackets to reveal identical t-shirts with a bequiffed lion rampant logo surrounded by the words 'Rednecks - Jockabilly'. I had no idea that they had these, as the Black Puma had printed them up in secret, and to see around fifteen of them in the audience was a real buzz. We rewarded them by playing almost all of the same fucking songs that they had heard at every other gig.

Once the gig was over, and we had mopped up our sweaty bodies, there was a slight feeling of relief as we had the whole weekend ahead of us, it was paid for, and we could now lapse into a drunken stupor. However, if truth be told, the addition of wives and girlfriends subdued the proceedings a little as some of us were badgered into dopey things like washing, eating some decent food and even (eek!) going for a walk outside the campsite. Never again. The whole Big Rumble experience is best enjoyed completely stoned and pissed for the duration, venturing only in a straight line between the caravan and the venue. Keep that other shit for family outings. I even 'cooked' a meal on one of the days, what a waste of good drinking time.

One of the bonuses of us not being face down in a puddle of beer for three days was an occasion, while out strolling, when I met Del from Fury. He told us that a band had dropped out of Sunday's line-up and offered us a second chance to perform. Although it was in the afternoon, it gave us a second chance to reach some of the punters who may have missed our Friday evening spot and, despite our general laziness, we did enjoy putting on a show when the occasion arose.

Maybe it was because most folks had been pissed for two days but our Sunday gig seemed to go down well and we played alongside a band who I felt shared that heavier edge (albeit in a more accomplished rockin' form) The Hellbillys. They were a fine bunch of yanks who were very friendly, even though a member of our band put the love touch on one of their girlfriends. The whole weekend was a great buzz, boozing, meeting other bands and (who knows) even shifting a few Rednecks singles but it would turn out to have been the peak of The Rednecks' career. Dark clouds of peeve and anger lay ahead.

Chapter 13:
What this world needs is a few less Rednecks.

As the man said (whoever the fuck 'the man' was) 'All rude things must come to an end' and despite the 'success' of our Fury EP (guffaw, guffaw!) The Rednecks were "rollin, rollin" to an undignified end. In retrospect it was almost a clean four-way split but leading up to our band's implosion was a rocky road.

I am convinced that most Psychobilly bands are run solely on friendship and a love for the music, alongside each member's desire to let it rip onstage. Lets face it, few bands other than the very top of the psycho pile make a living out of it. This may be a wild generalisation but I know that even members from bands at the height of their powers, such as The Guana Batz and Torment, still held down 'real' jobs. When you are changing into your stage gear in the unlit bogs of The Sir George Robey, after paying to get down to the big smoke, you have got to be in it for the buzz only. If it stops being fun and a good time on the road, then fucking forget it.

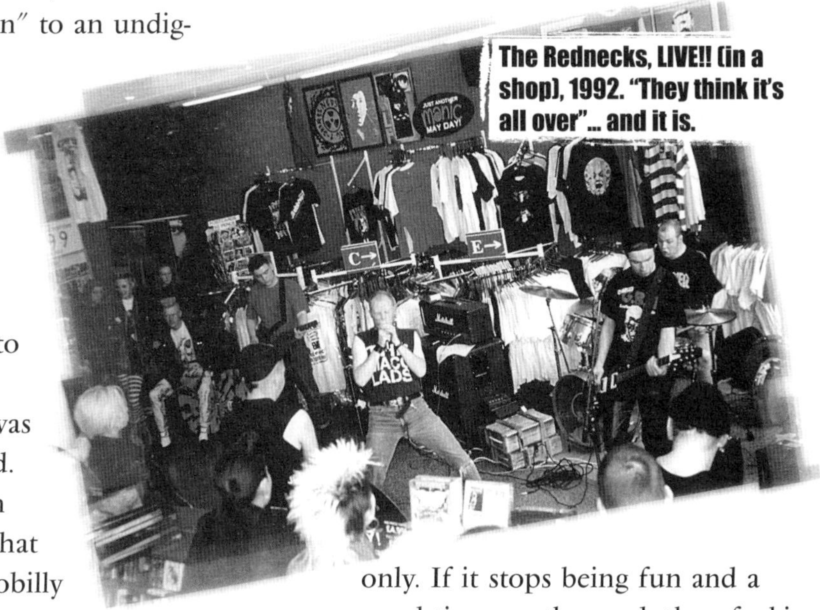

The Rednecks, LIVE!! (in a shop), 1992. "They think it's all over"... and it is.

The rot began to set in one chilly Saturday in January 1992. After the usual Hogmanay antics had faded, we dusted ourselves off and pegged it down to London for an all-day Psychobilly bonanza, at the aforementioned Robey in London's Finsbury Park, where The Klingonz had secured us a support gig. This venue was a real eye-opener as it consisted of a 'ye olde' London style pub with a separate room for mostly Psychobilly and Punk gigs. It also boasted the skankiest toilets in Britain which appeared to have the lethal combination of no windows, no plumbing and (often) no lights. The first time I visited, the bog was in a complete blackout and I just had to piss where I thought the urinal was. Judging by the splashing sound from the floor most people had the same problem. I then had to wait until someone opened the door before I could find my way out. Nonetheless, it was a cracking venue and it often offered psycho-alldayers with supping outside, in between bands, in its ramshackle beer garden. The place also had its share of soap-dodging crustie regulars an, on one occasion, a mate of mine was accosted by a gypsy woman who dragged him to her 'caravan' and would not let him out for two days in a marathon session of pikey-pokin'.

This gig was to provide yet more Rednecks disharmony and, again, we were travelling down separately. Kev and Stix came down by train on the day, Murray and his wife were opting for some guest house action and I came down on Glasgow's notorious 'Overnight Express' (cheap as fuck but sweaty, cramped and full of half-wits) with Bert, Tripney and Pat the Hat. We arrived in the capital at six in the morning and staggered off the bus like a quartet of bleary-eyed hunch-backs. After a quick visit to The Klingonz 'psycho-mansion' Gosterwood Palace, we caught the tube to Kensington to waste some time poking through their market complex of record shops and alter-native clothes emporiums.

While we window-shopped we were approached by a young fox who asked us if we would be willing to appear as extras in a low-budget movie her company were filming that very day. The film's provisional title was 'The Punk' and she thought we fitted the bill, especially with our matching biker's jackets that featured The Rednecks' skull 'n' flags logo. Very dapper. I have always been a full-on movie fanatic and I persuaded the others to agree, despite the fact that I had a mid-afternoon soundcheck way across town at the Robey.

At first we retired to a boozer... and waited. Then the girl returned with some producer type who agreed that we would be ideal for the scene but claimed that the crew were a bit behind schedule. He asked us to wait, so we continued supping. The girl then returned some time later and asked us all round to

The Rednecks promo blitz continues, 1992. Promoting our rockin' but unreleased classic, 'HuntShootFishFuck'.

their production office. We assumed that at last filming was now imminent but all they had for us were beer and excuses so we waited again. By this time I was due at the soundcheck but vainly chose to continue waiting, for the chance to be immortalised in a no-budget movie for a few seconds. Eventually after yet more excuses from the film crew the rest of the lads got pissed off with waiting, told the producer to forget it, and dragged me across town to fulfil my musical obligations.

Whe I arrived at the Robey, pissed, it was early evening and the rest of The Rednecks were mutinous. They had sat around expecting my arrival then attempted a soundcheck which had been a largely pointless exercise. I tried to brush their anger off in a cavalier fashion and get into a pre-performance mood but they just got even more pissed off when they discovered that I had wasted most of the day sitting around waiting for a micro-part in a no-name movie that would come to nothing. Despite this, the gig went well and after it I disappeared again with Tripney, Bert and Pat into the more cheerful company of the Klingz and their amigos. In retrospect not a smart move and, yet again, another fucked-up decision on my part which no doubt lit the spark of a future Rednecks' rebellion.

My next opportunity to piss the rest of the band off came a few months later when we were again invited back to Billy's club in Stoke, again propping up a bill with Demented Are Go and The Coffin Nails. I was travelling down in the van with Kev, Stix, a female acquaintance of mine and all the gear. Murray was again opting for a cosier car trip along with his wife and another couple while Big Bert and Tripney were whizzing down in Bert's wheels. Why we could not all cram in the van, like the old days, was beyond me but even now folks were looking for outlandish comforts like beds and showers.

Accompanied as I was with female company I intended to meet up with the other 'couples' for a B&B booking. Kev and Stix were sticking admirably to the old A/B plan (ie. kipping in the van). When we arrived, Tripney and Bert were already boozing so I believed it was important I started supping too. Glasses emptied, rounds were bought and by the time Murray and his posse appeared they were furious that I had kept them waiting and had not yet appeared at the bed and breakfast to book in. His wife and I immediately got into an argument but he merely glared menacingly.

I knew Murray had a foul temper, and was sure he was going to knock me out before the sound-check but it all blew over before the gig (I thought). Blissfully unaware, I carried on boozing and the gig whizzed by in a happy blur. The geezer flogging the bootleg Rednecks badges and two fine performances from Demented and Humongous and the boys was pretty much all I recall. As we trundled back home the next day sullen murmurs were hinting that, despite a great gig, the wheel nuts were popping off The Rednecks bandwagon.

In May 1992, The Rednecks' story drew to a close not with the sonic boom we would probably have liked but with something far nearer the low trump of a wet fart. Tower Records in Glasgow was Scotland's largest record store with a reputation for hosting major instore events from the likes of Bon Jovi, Wet Wet Wet, Kiss and Danzig. As an employee of the store, I was keen to add The Rednecks to this illustrious list and attempt a 'promo' event to publicise our throbbing red (vinyl) seven inch. In reality I knew instore bands always got a substantial booze rider and it meant an afternoon away from the till for me.

I had also organised a gig for The Klingonz in Glasgow one Friday night so I took the opportunity of asking them to headline an instore gig with us in support the following afternoon. I thought it would be a great chance to give Tower customers an afternoon of free Psychobilly while also introducing some unsuspecting Saturday shoppers to a burst of that unique Klingabilly sound. The Klingz were up for it so I got a PA booked, ordered all of their albums for sale on the day and set about publicising the event.

Now here seems to be the root of The Rednecks demise. Although the event appeared to be a solo effort on my part, this was mainly because I worked in the store and had ample time (company time that is) and resources to organise the whole thing. My mistake appears to have been that I did not 'consult' with the rest of the band in any great depth. In my mind what fucking consultation was needed, as I assumed that a weekend with The Klingonz, two gigs and a heap of free booze would be a blast. Unfortunately, not all my fellow 'necks agreed. Murray was up for it (have bass, will travel) but Kev and Stix thought the instore was a dopey idea.

In retrospect I had booked the gig without asking them all first but, again, I thought they would be keen to create a rockin' racket even if it was in the afternoon. At first there was almost a geetar and drums mutiny but I persuaded them to play as I had already advertised the gig and contacted the Rednecks' regulars. Then, in rehearsals for the instore there was mucho dissent that as it was an afternoon gig open to all ages the language would have to be toned down a bit (so 'Handjob Baby' was out). There was no such problems with The Klingonz set as they swear so regularly, and so quickly, that most of their cursing went over the punters' heads. Generally, in the Rednecks' camp, the petty shit was beginning to leave a bad taste (the pettiness, not the shit...perv fans).

And so it went on, surly communication before the gig and a litany of equipment and stage set-up moans and groans before we took to the stage on the Friday night, in support of The Klingonz, at a club called Nice 'n' Sleazy. I was on such a buzz (and pissed) that I failed to notice Kev, and particularly Stix, disillusionment. They had had enough but I was too busy to notice and along with The Klingz and the Kilsyth & Easterhouse crews we carried on partying.

And then...that was it! The instore the following day was the final nail in the coffin. The gig itself, I thought, went quite well. We bounced on to a make-shift stage in the T-shirt department in front of a sizable audience of jockabillies, the Klingz entourage and some bemused shoppers. I screamed my way through the first two songs before I discovered that the mike was unplugged (sabotage?... you decide!), then we left to make way for a live Klingonz tea-time treat. They really left the casual spectators reeling with their combination of visual splendour and klingabilly boogie. I was on a high as I had played two fine gigs in one weekend and had barely sobered up throughout. Kev and Stix came offstage, packed up and went home. If I had known that was to be our last gig perhaps we could have made some announcement but maybe that would have been too bullshit showbizzy. Nobody would really miss The Rednecks anyway and I just wanted to keep rocking.

Despite The Rednecks career farting to a close, I was in no mood to stop the rockin'. The Rednecks finale at The Klingonz/Tower Records instore gig was in May 1992 but mere weeks later we were due to support The Klingz again down at The Robey. I explained to the gigs's organisers that The Rednecks had undergone a name change but would still honour the booking. I then set about forming a new band... rapidly.

Kev was out of the scene (temporarily) and Stix was gone forever but despite our brief set-to at the Billy's gig, Murray and I still kept in touch and soon discussed forming a new band based on an Eighties Trash / Sixties Garage Punk vibe. We got on board Stu Cairns on guitar, a geezer who had been a Psychobilly along with us in the very early days in Glasgow but his school days love of Madness obviously never left him and he had returned to the way of the skins, eventually singing and playing guitar in a London Oi band. When he joined Murray and I he was in his sixties phase with an alarmingly healthy mop-top and a reverb-heavy guitar sound.

THIS IS TRASH... The Salem Dragsters, MkII, 1993. L-R: Bracko, Mark, Murray & Yoker Ian.

Also on guitar was Mark, a youthful modish type who Murray met through some East Kilbride connection. Mark was a little rusty at first but more importantly he was keen to bash out a lively garage racket and, in my books, enthusiasm and excitement are far more important than technical brilliance. Finally, as our skin-basher, we tracked down Yoker Ian. Ian was an ace drummer who had backed a number of local Psychobilly and Rockabilly bands and was comfortable with a more raw, stripped-down three or four piece kit. He regularly busked with Rock 'n' Roll bands on the street and helped complete our five-man Garage Punk explosion, the subtly monikered Salem Dragsters.

No sooner had we battered together a set list worth of songs than it was time to head for London. Yet again it was to be silliness on the travel front. Stuart was in London, Yoker Ian was in Germany and the rest of us were on the midnight express from Glasgow along with the Black Puma. When we reached the big smoke Stuart was easy enough to find but Ian appeared to be stuck in a transit van in Deutchland with Glasgow Rockabilly regulars The Cottonfield Boys.

I am sure most bands would not even leave home without their drummer but we (as always) ran our affairs with a roll of the dice and were soon at the venue, drummerless, and up for a sound-check. Luckily, to save us from looking a right bunch of tits, Mocker from The Klingonz offered to help us out and after listening to a few of the tunes he bashed the tubs for us as our special guest drummer. Thanks to The Mocker the gig went well but was, for obvious reasons, a little short on running time. The squeeze who was promoting the gig flipped her wig at our short set and forced us back onstage where we played a few of the songs again. The punters, too pissed to notice, cheered us on anyway. After that it was out to the beer garden for booze & acid. The Salem Dragsters were officially on the road, even though our actual skin-basher was stuck at German motorway services munching on a sausage (probably).

Unfortunately due to many varied reasons The Salem Dragsters, despite being probably the best band I was ever part of, never really got rolling. One main reason was my growing apathy with band life. Despite the very limited success of The Rednecks, I felt in a way I had achieved what I had wanted since

THE SALEM DRAGSTERS IN

ENTER THE DRAGSTERS

Early Salem Dragsters promo material, 1994.

boyhood, namely to be etched in vinyl for posterity without having to pay for it myself. Recently that achievement has been sidestepped by a lot of bands who can now burn their own CD's at home and release singles and albums with frightening regularity. While this is fine for promotional purposes, I still believe that having someone willing to place their faith in your band and invest in pressing up an official single or album is a far greater achievement ('Gawd bless yer Uncle Del'). After our single release I initially felt that the whole band thing was an anti-climax... and there lies the difference between your part-time rockers and your serious musos who constantly set new goals in their musical career.

Salem Dragsters contemplate a heavy touring schedule, 1994. L-R: Yoker Ian & Mark.

I always delivered the full whack when playing live but spending hours rehearsing and writing new songs became a drag (sic). As I was also one of the driving forces when it came to organising practice sessions, promoting the band and punting for gigs, all these elements became lax and slipshod. Rare gigs and infrequent rehearsals did not sit well with everyone and The Salem Dragsters personnel shifted like a weird shape-shifting thing.

Stu Cairns drifted off leaving Mark on his own in the guitar department. Kev Redneck then rejoined the fold to beef up the sound, then Mark moved to London leaving The Dragsters with three-quarters of the original Rednecks line-up. Yoker Ian also drifted off the radar so a workmate of mine, Andy G-Spot, took over on drumskin-bashing duties.

Andy was a modish, freakbeat fan who brought a more 60's sound to our meagre set and, with Kev now in string-bending overdrive, this was the tightest outfit I had screamed in front of since The Razorbacks. We re-tuned the set to thirty minutes of the finest psycho-sixties-garage-punk-raunchabilly, taking in a mix of decent originals, old favourites and trash 'n' nuggets cover versions. But again, the momentum faded and apart from a fine support slot with Tenpole Tudor, we fell under the Glasgow venue curse which consists of lots of multi-band line-ups where endless waves of no-name bands fight for a dwindling audience and a half-decent soundcheck. For five years we averaged one or two gigs a year... and then things got quiet. We never mentioned splitting up and have remained good mates so possibly, somewhere in the mists of time, we could still be coaxed out of retirement to wreak garage fury on some unsuspecting punters. Until then, all that remains for future generations is a two-track demo CD and a pop video featuring us miming frantically in a disused petrol station (on a bollock-freezing day) just outside the Scottish town of Shotts. Hillbilly indeed!

Aieee!! Baldness strikes the cruelest blow

In a direct parallel to The Salem Dragsters' faltering career my Psychobilly lifestyle (for want of a better description) was losing focus. I started to lose track of the new directions Psychobilly was taking in the mid-Nineties and travelled to far fewer gigs and weekenders. My jockabilly amigoes were also slipping from the scene as jobs, girlfriends and new wives also began to vie for their attentions while varying levels of baldness gripped the hairlines. My own barnet receded rapidly, retreating to a short flat-top, a skinhead and finally (that old favourite) constantly wearing a cap. I reacted by unleashing a rapidly changing combination of beards and sideburns.

Despite this, I knew deep down that I would never completely lose faith. Psychobilly has shaped my attitude and musical taste so strongly it can never be forgotten and many of my current mates and aquantancies still connect back in many ways to my time on the psycho scene. So much of my life still relates back to my first peek at King Kurt on TV, and my first spin of a Meteors album, that to dismiss Psychobilly as a teenage phase that I passed through would be (big, hairy) bollocks. A quick blast of a classic Psychobilly or Trash track can still set me miming frantically while wrecking wildly in front of the bedroom mirror like a complete tit.

From the mid-Mineties onwards, my Psychobilly moments were, however, a bit lean. I spent some time, along with

Cumbernauld old 'Billies. Still tokin', 1995. L-R: Raymie, Bracko & Johnny (the peeker).

my jock mates, down in London visiting The Klingonz at their psychobilly mansion. This pad was a psycho-version of 'The Young Ones' flat, right down to the healthy supply of scud-mags in the bog. I returned the favour when the band crashed at my flat, after a gig up in Glasgow, but (as I had a lady friend staying) I stashed all my porn to protect my puritan reputation (or in case they fired into them).

Another visitor to my concrete high-rise block was the mighty P. Paul Fenech. When The Meteors rolled into town with my mate Raymie on drums, we offered them a nights kip in the cement jungle that is Cumbernauld. Paul, his wife Michelle and a few of the Kattle bedded down at my flat while the rest of the Krew flaked out at Raymie's. Everything went well and they were great guests, even though it freaked me out a little that the man who started me off on the Psychobilly trail, as a spotty youth all those years before, was now in my pad. Especially in Cumbernauld, a place no one visits without good reason and certainly not a part of the country you would ever expect to find the Godfather of Psychobilly.

After The Meteors left town, Psychobilly bands seemed to leave Scotland off the map and Hemsby/Gt. Yarmouth was the only venue of choice where you could pack in the highest ratio of Psychobilly bands per journey south. The last weekender I attended was the 7th Big Rumble and an excellent weekend was spent with a good Glasgow turnout and some welcome company from other bands and their amigoes, especially a geezer called Big Motty who seemed to live, drink, fart (and smash windows) in our caravan all weekend.

Face-squeezing fun at the 7th Big Rumble, 1994. L-R: Tripmey, The Black Puma, Motty & Quentin.

The Glasgow scene almost drifted off the map but many of the old faces could still be found regularly at punk gigs in clubs like Nice 'n' Sleazy, The 13th Note and King Tut's Wah Wah Hut. Concerts by The Cramps in recent years have been almost rocker's reunions. Keeping the flame alive in Scotland seems to have rested with Rock 'n' Roll & Rockabilly bands such as King Voodoo. Kenny Mitchell from The Termites pressed on with a more Punk-influenced outfit called Ninebar but a few years ago unleashed a one-off Termites reunion tour which kicked off in Glasgow and was fucking excellent. It maintained their place as the 'Kings of Jockabilly' and gathered so many of the old Glasgow crew together that there was almost a tear in my eye.

That may have been an end to the story had a bizarre twist of fate not came my way. While operating my record & memorabilia stall at the market in my newly adopted home town in the winter of 2002, I spotted a big geezer flicking through records at another stall. His hair was down but immediately sussed him as a Psychobilly so I pulled out a copy of The Rednecks single (which I am still trying to flog... they are cramping up my loft space) and placed it on my stall. He noticed it and we soon got talking. We talked about bands and venues and our paths had obviously crossed before at gigs and events. Malc had been into psycho for many years and had the same interest in the Trash and Garage boom as well. He told me that the East Midlands region had once supported a booming psycho scene with crews from Retford, Lincoln, Mansfield, Ollerton and Worksop. The Retford Porterhouse was a main venue for psycho & trash bands even though it has since been converted into yet another cheesy disco palace (the fuckin' cheapskates have still left the 'Porterhouse' sign visible). I mentioned that a geezer we spent a lot of time with at gigs down south, Shug, was an ex-pat jock who lived somewhere round these parts and it turned out that he & Malc were close friends from years back and were still rockin along with fellow wrecker Slinger.

We met up around Christmas 2002 and I was pleased to find the Psychobilly faithful still in action, especially after the Glasgow scene drifted apart, but a bit shocked to think that almost ten years since the Big Rumble heydays we were out on the town supping ale. Unfortunately, for me, they all still have immaculately maintained quiffs while I am stuck with my baldy pate & breezers combination. A few months later I was back out with them again and even more stunned to find a healthy scene at The Charlotte in Leicester witnessing The Nekromantix live promoting their latest album on something approaching a major-label deal on Hellcat Records.

All good things most certainly come to those who wait and I strongly feel that the punters who keep Psychobilly going strong are those that keep on buying the records, keep on patronising gigs and keep bashing out an unholy racket in countless bands. Promoters, record labels, fanzines and companies like Raucous, Nervous & Spindrift have consistently pushed on through lean times to keep Psychobilly alive. Which is just as well as no other fucker would lend a hand unless they thought there was a quick buck in it. Psychobilly is, and has always been, kept alive by people who love the music & the lifestyle. Major companies who dipped their toe in the early-psycho scene cleared out quick when they realised that this was not going to be a scene the could exploit then cast aside when they had milked it for a some easy money (unlike 'baggy', 'grunge' and 'Brit pop').

To its credit, the Psychobilly scene has consistently moved forward despite being starved of the oxygen of publicity for almost two decades. I do not wish to unleash any whiff of conspiracy but what other musical genre has been so steadfastly ignored, and occasionally derided, by the UK music press for so long. These days mags like 'Kerrang!' will happily kiss the ass of any band from the Epitath or Hellcat stable, even those of a psycho persuasion, but if you had asked them to give a reasoned review of a Psychobilly album in the mid-Eighties they would have tore out their poodle-perms in indignation. 'Sounds' was the only UK music paper to offer any serious coverage of Psychobilly and Trash, including two legendary front covers featuring The Meteors and The Sting-Rays, and it popped its clogs years ago. Credit for keeping the scene publicised lands squarely at the creeper-clad feet of all the faithful who have continued bashing out fanzines, indie magazines and more recently some excellent web sites.

I do not really give a fuck if the mainstream music business really ever cared for Psychobilly or not but I do feel that many classic British psycho bands have been short changed and any major exposure they could have received, in print or on TV & radio, would only have proved to a wider audience that Psychobilly is an innovative and, more importantly, exciting sound. If the Americans and the Australians are willing to invest in Psychobilly on a larger scale why can't Brit music bigwigs get their finger out of their arse and sign something more than weak-assed rock bands and depressed public-school boys. If I had my way the British pioneers of Psychobilly would be sunning themselves by the pools of LA mansions, thumbing their way through wads of royalty cheques, sipping Merrydown from crystal glasses and blasting out enough Psychobilly on the hi-fi to piss of their neighbours. They deserve it.

Surprisingly the scene appears to be far more healthy on a global scale in the 21st century than it is in Britain. After the pioneering work done by early UK, Euro & US bands (hats off to Mad Sin, Batmobile, The Nekromantix, The Hellbillys and Elvis Hitler) the sickness has spread across the world with Psychobilly now booming in South America, Australia, Japan, Europe and further far flung corners of the planet. The USA scene also seems to be particularly strong with the spectre of Psychobilly seeping into every state. No doubt alerted many years back by the success of the Reverend Horton Heat, bigger labels such as Epitath and Sub Pop are willing to invest in psycho-influenced bands. Aussie rockers The Living End even appear on Warners, the record industry giants who introduced us to the snore-inducing delights of Simply Red and Chris Rea. Back in

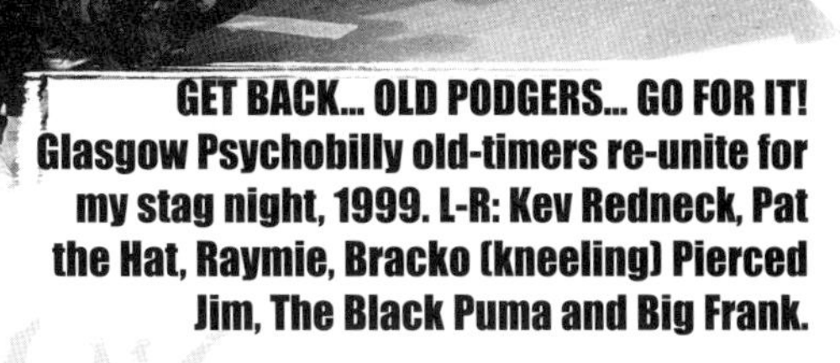

GET BACK... OLD PODGERS... GO FOR IT! Glasgow Psychobilly old-timers re-unite for my stag night, 1999. L-R: Kev Redneck, Pat the Hat, Raymie, Bracko (kneeling) Pierced Jim, The Black Puma and Big Frank.

the early Eighties a label like Warners would have shit their pants at the thought of The Meteors coming into the office to 'discuss terms' or panicked over the possibility of King Kurt staging a food fight in their staff canteen. In the live arena, promoters in America & Europe also seem to have no problem attracting punters for many regular weekenders and festivals featuring a variety of (mostly) home-grown psycho bands.

All this bodes well for a major Psychobilly renaissance in Britain - if only a new generation could pick up on it, and lets face it, if today's teens can be duped into reviving that tired British institution Goth then anything is possible. Generally though the kids, and bizarrely many major record labels, seem to look over the Atlantic for inspiration rather than dig in to the UK's fine pedigree of acts. If British kids find the phoney posturing of Limp Bizkit wild 'n' dangerous get them turned on to The Meteors for some real rockin' menace. And why not force feed some Demented Are Go to a new generation of teen rockers who think Tiger Army are the genesis of Psychobilly. The global psycho-phenomenon is a fantastic leap forward for this unique music genre but everyone should salute the early Psychobilly pioneers of the UK who bust their asses touring and recording, often on ultra-tight budgets, to keep the scene alive. Amen to that brothers & sisters!

When people say keep the faith it does actually have a real meaning. I may have drifted in and out of the scene over the years but I have never felt that being a Psychobilly at heart has left me. I know that there are thousands out there with far more dedication to the scene than me (and with far more depraved tales to tell) but on a personal level I feel I could never write off Psychobilly as a fad or phase which I went through. The music, the people and the lifestyle have made such an impression on me that, even as I trundle mercilessly towards forty, the sound of classic psycho tracks such as 'Wrecking Crew', 'Holy Hack Jack' and 'Curse of the Coffin' still give me a greater buzz than any other form of music. My friends, my musical tastes and even my personality all lead back to that one night when I witnessed King Kurt's first TV appearance then hunted down The Meteors debut. All I can ask for is that Psychobilly finally gets the recognition it deserves... and maybe that is just around the corner.

EPILOGUE

This entire book has been bashed out in the rare spare moments I have had since the birth of my baby son in 2001 and is perhaps not as long and as detailed as I would have liked. Another reason for some of the gaps and omissions has got to be my befuddled memory as I was almost consistently pissed and/or stoned throughout my Psychobilly days and far too fucked up most of the time to keep an accurate record of events. I apologise for this almost certainly muddled recollection but there you have it. "Better owt than nowt! - Keep wreckin!"

BRACKO

THANKS:

Normally thanks pages are a load of wank... so why break with tradition. On a genuine note, everyone below played some part in the creation of this book and to anyone I forgot... whoops! Dementia beckons!

THE INNER SANCTUM:

The Black Puma, Raymie, Tripney, Big Bert, Kev Redneck & Pat (the Hat).

BAND MEMBERS:

Murray, MaCaque, Kev (again), The G-Spot, Mark, Raymie (again), Gaz, Mick, Chris Hendrie, Stu Cairns, Yoker Ian, Mocker (one night only), Walter, Smiffy, Tally, James Blast, Heatnin' Plumbin' and that dopey bass-player from Kilsyth.

TO THOSE WE GAVE SUPPORT:

The Klingonz, Demented Are Go, Long Tall Texans, Duncan's Drunks, Self Destruct, The Termites, The Coffin Nails, The Lost Souls, The Hangmen, The Bad Men, Drunken State, The Hellbillys, Tenpole Tudor, many excellent Glasgow Punk bands (and a lot of shite ones).

HAYSEEDS & HILLBILLIES:

Eaky Broon, Twinger, Frank, Johnny (the Southside peeker), Danny Crainey, Steven Kelly, Scoob, Jaggy, Janice, Kay, Gordon Bennett, Sloss, Geordie Glen & Kilbride.

2ND EDITION THANKS TO

Carl, Big Keith, Dino, Cavan (Kev) Saunders, Darren (Eddie) Edwards, Jo (Alcoholic Rats), Loz (Hangmen), Alex Palao and everyone who coughed up for the 1st edition all around the globe. Extra special thanx to John Murray for providing the old-skool snaps on pages 18, 40 & 88.

GLASGOW PSYCHOBILLY OLD-TIMERS & ROCKABILLY KATS:

Quentin, Kathie Pumette, Scotty, Watty, Ali Goldenhour, Moorsy, Eddie Barr, Kev the Gerbil, Easterhouse Ian, Spotty John, Eds, Kenny Mitchell, Shavings, Susan (Bet Lynch), Paul, Bruno, Brendan, Tonto, Shorty, Big Joe, Valerie, Mish, Woodsy, Queen of the Teds, Miss Devine, Big Angie, Susan (page 3), Baldragon Brian, Dougie the Banker, Beardsy, Jason, Big Gary, Brad and all the other psychos from Paisley, Uddingston and anywhere with a Glasgow postcode.

TWO-WHEEL BURNERS:

Tracy, Lorna, George, Ritchie, Shane, Jack, Louise, Gordon, Robin (are ye knobbin'), Stripey, Whiit, Graham, George, My Sweet Wife and all the other Scottish scooter trash who spent time with the Glasgow Vespa Club.

SPREADING THE PSYCHO DISEASE ACROSS BLIGHTY:

Shug, Malc, Slinger, Butch, Ross and the Dundee Psycho Krew '83-'86, Motty, Adam, Gally, John & The Chook.

HELPING MAKE 'LET'S WRECK' A REALITY:

Jo Shalton (Psychodame), Wayne Beauchamp & Roy Williams.

AND FINALLY:

P. Paul Fenech and all Meteors past & present for making Psychobilly a way of life and without whom I would probably still be listening to 1980's Pop shite and dressing like a poseur. Thank you!